Conversations with Anthony Giddens

Conversations with Anthony Giddens

Making Sense of Modernity

Anthony Giddens and Christopher Pierson

Stanford University Press
Stanford, California
1998

Stanford University Press
Stanford, California
© 1998 Anthony Giddens and Christopher Pierson
Originating publisher: Polity Press, Cambridge
  in association with Blackwell Publishers Ltd.
First published in the U.S.A. by
  Stanford University Press, 1998
Printed in Great Britain
Cloth ISBN 0-8047-3568-9
Paper ISBN 0-8047-3569-7
LC 98-60918
This book is printed on acid-free paper.

Contents

Preface   vii

Acknowledgements   xi

The Sociology of Anthony Giddens:
  An Introduction (*Martin O'Brien*)   1

Interview One: Life and Intellectual Career   28

Interview Two: The Sociological Classics and Beyond   52

Interview Three: Structuration Theory   75

Interview Four: Modernity   94

Interview Five: From the Transformation of
  Intimacy to Life Politics   118

Interview Six: Politics Beyond Left and Right   151

Interview Seven: World Politics   170

Centre Left at Centre Stage   194

Contents

The Politics of Risk Society 204

Beyond Chaos and Dogma . . . 218

Risks, Scares, Nightmares 227

Preface

As Martin O'Brien's introductory essay makes clear, Anthony Giddens is something of a social science phenomenon. Over a quarter of a century of unrelenting productivity, he has become established as one of the world's most authoritative and widely cited social theorists. His interests are remarkably diverse, from the driest of Continental philosophy to the therapy-speak of the self-help manual, and his work builds upon a critical engagement with an extraordinary array of texts from within and way beyond the canon of the social sciences. He has helped to develop a whole new lexicon with which we can grasp what it means to live in the rapidly changing world of modernity: structuration, practical consciousness, time-space distanciation, manufactured risk, life politics. As if this were not quite enough, Giddens has also made the time to co-found his own publishing house, head up the new Faculty of Social and Political Sciences at the University of Cambridge, and still bear witness to the failure of his beloved Spurs football team to recreate the successes of his north London youth.

In 1997, Giddens took up his most significant challenge as Director of the London School of Economics. Giddens has a very clear view of the special role of the LSE. The School has always been engaged in a special way with the real world of politics and policy-making, especially in periods of systematic reform. In recent years, Giddens has himself shown an increasing interest in and engagement with the world of mainstream politics and, since arriving at the LSE, has rapidly set about creating the links that will make the School's 'special relationship' with the wider world of political practice work. That the arrival of a new and activist Director at the LSE should be so closely followed by the election of the first centre-left government for a generation has made for exciting times. And Giddens's belief in the importance of the 'radical centre' and of a 'Third Way' that goes 'beyond right and left' has made him a popular and influential figure at the top of the New Labour hierarchy.

The interviews which make up the greater part of this book were all conducted within months of Giddens's arrival at the LSE and in the aftermath of the New Labour success of 1 May 1997. They seek to cover the full range of his thought since the early 1970s, beginning with his engagement with the makers of 'classical' sociology and concluding with his thoughts on the nature of world politics under 'reflexive modernity'. The style is conversational and technical jargon is kept to a minimum. I have tried to ask the questions which any interested reader might pose and left Giddens to answer in his own, uniquely clear and concise voice.

Giddens remains a controversial figure. His critics insist that his work is not just wide-ranging and diverse but shallow and eclectic. They argue that he never stays in one spot long enough either to be pinned down or to establish the truth of what (for them) remain largely unsubstantiated conjectures. But even his fiercest critics would find it hard to deny that Giddens's

work fizzes with challenging ideas and provocative suggestions. Others will simply want to admire and learn from this
intellectual *tour de force*.

Chris Pierson
Nottingham
March 1998

Acknowledgements

The editors and publishers wish to thank the following for permission to use copyright material:

London Review of Books for Anthony Giddens, 'Risks, Scares, Nightmares' (review: 'Why sounding the alarm on chemical contamination is not necessarily alarmist'), *London Review of Books*, 5.9.96;

Polity Press for Anthony Giddens, 'The Politics of Risk Society' ('Risk Society: the Context of British Politics') in Jane Franklin, ed., *The Politics of Risk Society* (1997) pp. 23–34;

New Statesman Ltd for Anthony Giddens, 'Beyond chaos and dogma. . .', *New Statesman*, 31.10.97; and Anthony Giddens, 'Centre left at centre stage', *New Statesman*, May 1997, Special edition.

Every effort has been made to trace the copyright holders but if any have been inadvertently overlooked the publishers will be pleased to make the necessary arrangement at the first opportunity.

The Sociology of Anthony Giddens: An Introduction

Martin O'Brien

Anthony Giddens is one of the leading British sociologists of the post-war period. His writings span more than three decades of social and political change and have been at the forefront of the development of sociological theory and practice in the 1980s and 1990s. His interpretations of the classical sociological traditions have been a central pillar of much undergraduate and postgraduate teaching in sociological theory for twenty years (and continue to be so) and his imaginative reconstruction of sociology's central concerns has stimulated academic debate and intellectual controversy in equal measure. He is an agenda-setting social theorist, a virtual one-man publishing industry, and a political philosopher of growing influence, and he has now taken on the professional challenge of directing the London School of Economics and Political Science in the uncertain era of the first Labour government since the 1970s.

In introducing the extraordinary breadth of Giddens's thinking to the new reader, I will focus on the outlines of his overall project, rather than on the critical details of any of its specific

aspects. In particular, I will emphasize the connections between the different strands of his diverse output in order to
provide a conceptual map of his theoretical and philosophical
thinking. In this way, I want both to give a sense of the importance of his work and to disclose some of the critical questions that his reconstruction of sociology raises. I begin with
some comments on Giddens's understanding of the discipline
of sociology before going on to sketch in some of the main
contours of his work.

The sociological enterprise

According to Giddens, sociology is a special kind of intellectual discipline. Unlike physical scientists, a sociologist
seeks to understand a world that is already understood by
its members. The 'objects' of sociological inquiry – what
people say and do, what they believe and desire, how they
construct institutions and interact with each other – are
unlike the objects of natural sciences, such as physics, chem-
istry or biology, in so far as people's actions and interactions, their beliefs and desires, are a central feature of the
world that the sociologist investigates. Moreover, this world
cannot be reduced to one 'correct' set of meanings or explanatory system. The social world is irreducibly characterized by competing and sometimes conflicting frames of
meaning, understandings, and patterns of belief. When
physicists dispute with each other about whether (and why)
the universe is expanding, they are disputing the single,
unique cause and character of the basic physical relationships between energy and matter. When sociologists dispute
with each other about whether (and why) society is divided
by relationships of class, gender, ethnicity or personality,

they are disputing the complex intersections between different layers of social experience and action. Sociologists must develop alternative kinds of explanation for each of these social forces because there is not one unique cause and character of the basic relationships between individuals and society.

To take another example, a chemist, in seeking to understand the properties of water, need not wonder whether some atoms of hydrogen *intended* to bond with some atoms of oxygen to produce a pond, a lake or an ocean; even less what it *means* to the different hydrogen atoms to get together with oxygen atoms to make water. A sociologist, on the other hand, is faced precisely with the problem that people have motivations and purposes for doing what they do, that (mostly) they know why they are doing the things they do, and that the meaning of their actions and interactions is, at least to some degree, transparent to them. Whilst the hydrogen and oxygen atoms did not intend to produce the lake or the ocean, people manifestly do intend to get married or divorced, live in town or countryside, work for wages or employ others to do so for them. It may be that some people get married or go to work in spite of the fact that they do not want to, but they could not marry or work unintentionally. Thus, unlike the natural sciences, sociology must seek to understand the relationships between people's intentions and purposes and the character of the social world they inhabit.

The sociological problem, however, is yet further complicated by the fact that sociologists belong to the world they research: they employ the same kinds of everyday routines to manage their lives and engage in meaningful actions and interactions with the people and institutions which are the objects of their study. The social being of the sociologist, including what the sociologist knows about the objects of her research, is inescapably mediated by the social world she inhabits. In accounting for that world the sociologist must draw upon the common-sense understandings and the socially embedded beliefs and meanings that make it what it is. Whereas the chemist in my earlier example does not and cannot draw upon the hydrogen atom's account of its *physical* existence, the sociologist *must* draw upon people's ordinary accounts of their *social* existence. The sociologist is first and foremost an ordinary member of the world she investigates whose explanations of that world, like those of every other individual within it, are part and parcel of its basic character.

In this respect, the sociologist's task – of explaining how the social world works or how and why a society is organized in one way rather than another – appears, at first sight, as a second-order account, or gloss, on how all of us ordinarily explain the world for ourselves. After all, if people know what they are doing and why, at least most of the time, if they know and understand the causes and consequences of their daily, routine activities, then the sociologist's account merely adds to the total number of explanations of the world that can be given and is neither more nor less insightful, rigorous or accurate than any other. What, then, does the sociologist do that might lead anyone to suppose that a professional sociologist's account of the world had any value?

Giddens's response is to propose that sociology performs a 'double hermeneutic': it spirals in and out of the knowledges of everyday life. Its fate is always to become entangled in the common-sense accounts by which people explain their world. Concepts and ideas that have been extensively developed in sociology, notes Giddens – like 'social status', the 'charisma' of religious and political leaders, or 'moral panics' – are now widely used in the media and in ordinary, everyday discussions. Social research into divorce rates, the distribution of health and illness, income and lifestyle, the effects of the media, patterns of family formation and much more is now a central pillar of local and national policy formulation. Sociological knowledge is destined to become 'what everyone knows' because sociological knowledge is precisely one of the main means by which members of modern society come to understand and account for the workings of that society. Sociological knowledge enters into, becomes a part of and helps to transform the very world that it seeks to explain and analyse (see Giddens, 1996: 4–5, 77). In this respect, the sociological enterprise is a critical endeavour: it draws upon the ordinary meanings shared by people in society but reformulates and expands them in order to assist in the process of positive social change. It is a conscious exercise in what Giddens calls social reflexivity (which I explain in more detail below): the reflective application of knowledge *about* the social world to meet the challenges of new circumstances and conditions *in* the social world. Stated thus, the idea appears alluringly simple, but its emergence in Giddens's work and its diffusion throughout professional sociology have involved a long and arduous expedition through the jungles of classical and contemporary sociological thought.

Settling accounts with the classics

Giddens began writing and publishing on classical sociological theory in the late 1960s. At the time, the discipline's understanding of the works of classical theorists (notably

Marx, Weber and Durkheim) was dominated by American traditions – and, in particular, by the writings of Talcott Parsons. Not only were these traditions dominant in *interpreting* the classics, they also tended to be dominant in determining how these should be applied to practical problems such as deviance, health and illness, mass media effects, or social integration, for example. During the 1960s Giddens addressed both of these tendencies simultaneously. In relation to the first, he reconsidered the sociologies of Marx, Weber, Durkheim and Simmel. In relation to the second, he expended a great deal of energy on reconsidering the sociology of suicide. The choice of this problem as a vehicle through which to explore sociological theory was significant in a number of ways. It was significant because it led Giddens to a systematic reappraisal of the work of Émile Durkheim – whose own study of *Suicide* in 1897 (Durkheim, 1897) had represented an attempt to cast the new discipline of sociology as a positive, objective science of society. It was significant also because, as Durkheim had recognized, the study of suicide exposes a fundamental theoretical task of sociological inquiry. That task is to reveal how a social science which deals with social forces, social structures and social action can understand an event that, commonsensically, appears intensely personal and private. A third way in which the problem of suicide was significant was that, in his treatment of the topic, Giddens was forced to address a radical division within sociology between two apparently opposed and mutually exclusive approaches to the study of a common problem – the 'positivist' approach and the 'phenomenological' approach – representing two distinct sociologies inhabiting the post-war academy (see Dawe, 1970).

In brief, the positivist approach, drawing on Durkheim's

methods and guidance, attempted to show the objective correlations between rates of suicide and various external factors such as urban isolation (Sainsbury, 1955). The phenomenological approach, drawing on the philosophy of Edmund Husserl, investigated how the event of a death is given the subjective meaning of 'suicide', under what circumstances and with what consequences. Whilst the positivist view accepts official data on suicide rates as presenting, more or less, an accurate picture of its social reality, the phenomenological view undermines this idea by showing that cultural and subcultural factors influence whether any particular death will or will not be classified as suicide – either officially or otherwise (see Douglas, 1967). The 'two sociologies' division, in relation to the suicide problem, can be summed up in the form of two contrasting questions: is the sociological concept of suicide equivalent only to what is officially recorded as suicide by coroners and other functionaries? Alternatively, is it the task of sociology to probe the cultures and subcultures in which people understand and give personal significance to deaths as suicidal events?

In spite of expending much intellectual energy on this conundrum, Giddens's approach to the specific question of suicide in sociological theory has not been widely adopted by the social science community, partly because the analytical problem of suicide dropped off sociology's intellectual agenda. But his exposure to the problems that it throws up have reverberated throughout his work ever since. From the early 1970s, the suicide problem begins to drop off Giddens's own theoretical agenda and he takes up, instead, some of the broader theoretical issues that were raised by his encounter with it. In particular, the effort to interweave the positivist strand of Durkheim's thought with the phenomenological strand of Husserl's philosophy, although often not explicit, characterizes his writings throughout the 1970s and early 1980s.

In 1971, Giddens published *Capitalism and Modern Social Theory*, a book which remained his best-known work for some ten years and which – remarkably, given the numerous texts on the same topics that have appeared since – remains one of the most valuable sources on Marx, Weber and Durkheim. The book signalled the beginning of an extensive assessment of the complex layers of sociological theory in which Giddens is still engaged. In 1972 two related books appeared. One was an edited collection of Durkheim's writings (Giddens, 1972a), the other a short reflection on Max Weber's social and political writings (Giddens, 1972b). The next year saw the publication of *The Class Structure of the Advanced Societies* (Giddens, 1973), which was followed in 1974 by an edited collection on positivism and sociology (Giddens, 1974) and a collection on élites in British society (Giddens and Stanworth, 1974). Throughout this time Giddens was also busy writing articles for the professional press and in 1977 a collection of these essays appeared under the title *Studies in Social and Political Theory* (Giddens, 1977). These essays extended Giddens's treatment of the sociological classics and also engaged with other important and emerging traditions in social science – represented by, amongst others, Talcott Parsons and structural functionalism, Jürgen Habermas and critical theory, and Harold Garfinkel and ethnomethodology. In this period of theoretical and philosophical reflection, Giddens established the basis on which his later writings would propose a new sociological paradigm, *structuration theory*, whose outlines were tentatively hinted at in *New Rules of Sociological Method* (Giddens, 1976).

The title of this (1976) book is instructive for several reasons. Like Giddens's earlier focus on the suicide problem in sociology, the title of the 1976 book recalls the significance of Émile Durkheim to contemporary sociology. In 1895, Durkheim published his statement of what sociology *should* be in *The Rules of Sociological Method* (1895). For Durkheim, sociology is a systematic, disciplined, empirical science which treats the world as a source of objective data, comparable to the natural sciences and uninfluenced by the subjective beliefs and intentions of its members. For Giddens, in contrast, renewing sociology's outlook in the second half of the twentieth century requires that the subjective be brought back into the sociological fold – although in ways not envisaged by Durkheim. In short, for Giddens, sociology *should* attend to the world as a world that holds meaning and personal significance for its members, whose intentions, in one way or another, are central to sociological understanding. Otherwise, the discipline has no hope of explaining how each individual contributes to and helps to shape the collective history of society. *New Rules of Sociological Method* is at the same time an acknowledgement of the importance of Durkheim to Giddens's sociology and a settling of accounts with the Durkheimian tradition. Although the focus of the book is a critique of interpretative (or, loosely, phenomenological) sociologies, it is also a conscious acknowledgement of the need to go beyond Durkheim. After the publication of *New Rules*, a fresh chapter in Giddens's sociology begins and his new paradigm, *structuration theory*, is given its first systematic outline, three years later, in *Central Problems in Social Theory* (Giddens, 1979).

The theory of structuration

I have spent some time on Giddens's relationship to Durkheim's sociology, in particular, because it is central to his – or any – proposed reconstruction of the discipline. This is not to say that other classical sociologists – Marx and Weber, in particular – have not been important in his work, for they have. But Durkheim is the most important classical influence in structuration theory because his legacy leads Giddens to adopt a highly formal and abstract idea of 'social structure'. Whereas Marx, for example, described the structures of the capitalist system often in the most vivid and graphic detail – the factories, the slums and warrens, the engines of production, the opulence of the bourgeois class, the inevitable denigration and degradation of the proletariat, the formation of working-class movements and parties, and so on – Durkheim described structures indirectly, by analogy with the cells and organs of living bodies. Social structures were held together by the glue of 'social bonds' that were only visible to the sociologist abstractly – as more or less stable and ordered patterns of social integration. Giddens takes up a comparable formalist approach, but he argues that the concept of 'structure' in itself is of no use to sociology and that sociologists should speak of the 'structuring properties' of social interaction as media through which people achieve their purposes and goals.

If sociology is to understand the world as a world that both holds meaning for its members and is, at least in part, reproduced and transformed by them, then any sociological account of that world must recognize, so Giddens argues, that ordinary people's own accounts of it are themselves sociologies of a kind. Sociological knowledge and understanding are not the sole privilege of professional sociologists. People's routine behaviour both exposes and expresses the importance of sociological knowledges in the conduct of everyday life. Conversational rules, behavioural expectations or intimate interpersonal rituals, for example, are embedded in knowledge about how and why social life happens: who speaks or is silent and when, who stands or sits and why, who belongs or does not and where, who is revered or reviled and how – these are mundane constituents of everyday sociologies. Knowledge (however partial or fragmented it may appear) of how the social world works is embedded in the day-to-day actions and interactions of people living out their lives. It forms 'practical sociologies' that people use without, usually, consciously thinking about them. Such knowledge of how the world works is analogous to the rules of language use. Competent speakers of a language can use rules of grammar in order to communicate with each other but they do not need to make their grammatical knowledge an explicit feature of what they are saying. Indeed, if speakers and hearers always had to establish rules of grammar every time they communicated something, they would communicate very little at all. In using rules of grammar in order to communicate what they intend, speakers unintentionally reproduce them as rules of grammar. When I speak, my intention is to communicate a meaning and I may manipulate certain grammatical rules in order to make what I say more plausible, convincing or poetic, for example. However, whilst I may consciously orient to grammatical rules in order to realize my intentions, it cannot be said that my intentions include the reproduction of those grammatical rules. The reproduction of the rules of grammar is, from the point of view of my use of them, an *unintended consequence* of my effort to communicate a meaning.

Comparably, suggests Giddens, people also know 'rules' of social action and interaction that they do not need to formulate explicitly in order to live in society or to deal with social institutions. People draw on rules of action and interaction as resources that enable them to get things done on an everyday level. But this 'drawing on' has the consequence of reproducing those rules as structuring properties of their action and interaction. The apparent objectivity of the social world, the ways that it appears, from the point of view of any individual, ordered and rule-governed, are in reality an unintended consequence – an outcome neither premeditated nor designed by any one person or group – of the routinized practices that all individuals must employ in order to conduct their daily affairs.

Giddens does not deny that there are differences between rules of language use and social rules. His point is that the structuring properties of social action, like the rules of language use, are not only *constraints* on what can and cannot be achieved: social structures are not simply 'facts' that are external to or constraining upon the use that people make of them. Rather, they are conditions *of* social action that are reproduced *through* social action. In simplified form, this is what Giddens means when he writes:

> As I shall employ it, 'structure' refers to 'structural property', or more exactly, to 'structuring property', structuring properties providing the 'binding' of time and space in social systems. I argue that these properties can be understood as rules and resources, recursively implicated in the reproduction of social systems. Structures exist paradigmatically, as an absent set of differences, temporally 'present' only in their instantiation, in the constituting moments of social systems. (Giddens, 1979: 64)

The elaboration of structuration theory after 1979 takes some very complex and divergent routes. It is pitched against

Marxist sociologies of social change in *A Contemporary Critique of Historical Materialism. Volume 1: Power, Property and the State* (1981). Here, Giddens rejects the linear view of historical progress proposed by Marx – in which one mode of production inevitably gives way to another under the combined weight of its internal contradictions and a revolutionary class itching to overthrow existing conditions. Instead, Giddens develops a novel typology of social systems as arrangements of time-space relations – a theme that is extended in *The Constitution of Society* (1984), which is the formal (and, at least so far, final) statement of structuration theory. In brief, each historically located society encodes relations of time and space in its institutions, habits and practices. Social action of any kind is always situated *in* time and space but it also gives substance *to* time and space. In premodern societies, time and space are connected intrinsically to 'place'. Activities which occur at particular times – working, exchanging goods and services, even conversing – all transpire in limited and tightly bounded spatial contexts. The 'when' of activity is intimately connected to the 'where' of activity. In the modern world, in contrast, time and space are organized independently of each other: today, economic exchanges may take place across continents and time zones at the press of a computer key; telecommunications media make it possible to converse across vast distances and also to beam images of events from any one part of the world onto a screen virtually anywhere else in the world instantaneously or, as in *Match of the Day*, in endless replay. Time and space in the globalized modern world have been 'disembedded' from their traditionally local contexts of action. All social action occurs *in* time and space but the ways that time and space are organized *through* social action differs between modern and traditional societies.

Structuration theory is also applied to the question of the state and state violence in *The Nation State and Violence* (1985) (volume 2 of *A Contemporary Critique of Historical Material-ism*) and underpins diverse essays on contemporaneous so-ciological problems – including questions of ideology, space and time, revolution, social class, and power. At this stage of his writings, however, the question of the 'modern' becomes increasingly and explicitly central to Giddens's project. In fact, the later texts that are addressed specifically to this question, which I discuss next, are all rooted in the concepts and per-spectives put forward as the theory of structuration during the late 1970s and early 1980s.

Are we modern?

The idea that the world today is a 'modern' world is an em-bedded part of common-sense ways of thinking: it seems an obvious, indisputable fact. By all common-sense measures and standards, the contemporary world is incomparably modern, more intensively and extensively modern than early twentieth-century modernist artists and architects could have dreamed. Any simple comparison between life in the 1990s and life in the 1890s would suggest that there have been very many technological and social developments. Jet engines, video-recorders, microwaves, computers, nuclear power, space shuttles, genetic manipulation, a welfare state (for the time being), television, antibiotics, and so on all appear to confirm how much more complex, sophisticated and advanced is the world today than in the past. In comparison to the 1890s, then, life in the 1990s appears to be indisputably 'modern', so much so, in fact, that for some it is even more than modern, it is 'post-modern'.

But what is it to be 'modern'? What makes contemporary society more modern than the societies of our forebears? Our great-grandparents themselves believed that they were modern in comparison to their own forerunners. In what ways is society today so different from its past that we can claim to be modern *in contrast* to them? In some version or another, these questions have underpinned a very large part of the discipline of sociology: working out the unique characteristics of the present *vis-à-vis* the past has been central to sociology's understanding of itself. In a series of books addressed specifically to this question (Giddens, 1990; 1991; Beck, Lash and Giddens, 1994) Giddens's contribution to this understanding has been to make that uniqueness – the distinction of the present from the past – one of the central problematics of contemporary sociology. According to Giddens, the modernity of the world, what it is to *be* modern, is precisely the social arrangement of contemporary society as a world that has superseded its past, as a society that is not bound by the traditions, customs, habits, routines, expectations and beliefs that characterized its history. Modernity is an historical condition of difference; in one way or another a displacement of everything that has gone before. Note, here, that Giddens is not saying that there are no longer any traditions. Nor does he claim that people do not believe things that were believed by our forebears. On the contrary, Giddens proposes that the world today is a 'post-traditional' world to the extent that uncountable traditions, beliefs and customs mingle with each other. In this world, as Durkheim had claimed in 1898, no one tradition can hope to hold sway and no one customary mode of action can stand as the foundation for living one's life in the complex and ever-changing circumstances of the present. Traditions and customs, beliefs and expectations, today are adaptable, bendable, 'plastic' resources in a globalized, cosmopolitan world of intersecting cultures and life-styles. Thus, the modern world does not bring about the death of tradition. Instead, it locates and contextualizes traditions as alternative contexts of decision-making and as alternative sources of knowledge, value and morality. If once we lived in a traditional world, today we live in a world of traditions. In simplified form, this is what Giddens intends when he writes: 'Where the past has lost its hold, or becomes one "reason" among others for doing what one does, pre-existing habits are only a limited guide to action; while the future, open to numerous "scenarios", becomes of compelling interest' (1994: 92–3).

This transformation of tradition is unique to modernity. It is central to the distinction between the modern form of society and the premodern form of society and is institutionalized through the former's bureaucratic, commercial and technological systems. Although, today, the transformation is more clearly visible than ever before, this is because its long-term consequences are now more extensively experienced and more intensely engaged. Our great-grandparents were, indeed, modern but their society comprised a form of 'simple modernization' whereas, today, we have entered an age of 'reflexive modernization'. This term means that the contemporary era is characterized by a high degree of what Giddens calls 'social reflexivity'. Social reflexivity refers to a society where the conditions in which we live are increasingly a product of our own actions and, conversely, our actions are increasingly oriented towards managing or challenging the risks and opportunities that we ourselves have created. In earlier stages of history, human beings lived in conditions that were dependent to a large degree on external forces. The rhythms of the seasons, the cycles of night and day, the extremes of weather and the impenetrability of natural environments (the depths of the ocean or the heights of the skies, for example) comprised external limit points to human action. In our own society, night and day or the rhythms of the seasons are arbitrary temporal divisions in the context of a twenty-four-hour, three-hundred-and-sixty-five-day-a-year global economy. The depths of the oceans and the heights of the skies are resources that provide marine food or enable sea and air mobility and cable and satellite communication.

Furthermore, what used to be 'limits' to social action are now saturated with the consequences of that action. On the bottom of the ocean and in the outer limits of the atmosphere the environmental consequences of modern industrial society continue to accumulate. Whether one believes in the reality of global warming or not it cannot be denied that the air we breathe, the water we drink and the food we eat are saturated with the chemical contents of industrial society. If the meteorological office issues urban air pollution warnings, if the labels on our food list the (known) chemical additives in what we eat and if the water that pours from the tap is, variously, filtered, chlorinated and fluoridated, then it must be acknowledged that the environmental conditions of modern society are heavily mediated by the technological and expert systems of that society. Today, hardly any aspect of what used to be 'nature' escapes the influence of human technological and social inventiveness. From beef production to human reproduction, from nature reserves to 'experimental' sheep, from rivers running with oestrogen to valleys dusted with nuclear radiation, human beings live in environments of our own creation: environments that are no longer simply a constraining *limit to* what we can do but are increasingly *infused with* what we do. Where premodern societies faced the threat of natural risks, modern society faces the threat of manufactured risks –

risks to personal and planetary life that arise from the way
that we live today.

The modernity of the world comprises all of these things
– it is a characteristic less of any *particular* technology, institution or belief system than of the seemingly limitless opportunities and risks that contemporary societies appear to
offer. The modern technoscientific culture has cloned life
and revolutionized agriculture, it has reduced the world to a
few hours' flying time and photographed volcanoes from
space, it has introduced the microchip into the daily routines of millions of people and automated everything from
acquiring money from a hole in the wall to 'neutralizing' an
enemy with an (often not so) 'smart' missile. Contemporary
scientific and bureaucratic procedures have provided us with
both central heating and global warming, with two-minute
microwave meals and ten-year-incubated CJD. The wonders
of the world are matched step for step by the horrors of the
world in every domain of life from eating potentially dangerous meat to swimming in the sun-kissed waters of polluted
seas.

The peculiarly modern character of this paradox – the means
of sustaining our collective life is the major threat to planetary (and, therefore, collective) life – is repeated in each individual's relationships to modern society. Whereas in
premodern times my relationship to society, or, in other words,
my social identity, was constrained and limited by tradition,
kinship and locality, today this relationship is much more
ambiguous. I am surrounded by traditions of every conceiv-
able kind, I no longer inhabit the locality of my birth, and my
name – and the particular kinship connections it ostensibly
denotes – means nothing at all to readers of this text. Here, I
am a name on a page; there, I am a web-site address; elsewhere I am a national insurance number in a government com-

puter. My relationship to modern society – my social identity – has become unglued from the contexts, communities and expectations that once circumscribed my (and your) knowledge of who I am and how I live. Today, I am responsible and liable for my own identity. No longer bound by external reference points, my identity is a moving projection through the complex social and institutional contours of a globalized cultural system. In this world, all individuals must strive to reconcile the modern paradox for themselves by undertaking a 'reflexive project' of the self: each person is required to steer his or her own, individual course between the threats and the promises of modern society.

Yet, this risky scenario is not only a source of anxiety. True, the pace and diversity of contemporary social life, the uncertainty about the impact of sophisticated technologies like genetic engineering and the environmental problems of polluting societies may create conditions for widespread apprehension and psychological turmoil. At the same time, their very social visibility indicates that people are contributing to a redefinition of what modern society should be like: how animals should be treated, how pollution should be tackled, how different cultures should interact. The public resonance of questions relating to ethical matters – human and animal rights, the responsibilities of rich nations to poor nations, the status and social organization of social differences of sexuality, ethnicity, embodiment or gender, for example – indicates that modern society, no less than traditional society, continues to encounter and struggle over issues of moral conduct. This struggle, which Giddens refers to as a process of 'remoralization' of social life, suggests that politics today remains as salient as ever but the foundations of contemporary political action have undergone some profound changes. No longer appealing to socialist or neo-liberal traditions in

order to ground politics in morality, the new politics of reflexive modernity is moving, in the title of Giddens's (1994)
major work on political philosophy, *Beyond Left and Right*
(volume 3 of *A Contemporary Critique of Historical Materialism*).

The personal and the political

The rapid transformations that characterize the modern
world are not simply things that are 'out there', beyond the
experiences, intentions and desires of ordinary people. The
concept of modernity refers to the private and passionate as
well as the public and rational. For example, few would disagree that the languages of intimacy have undergone some
profound changes in recent times: 'Wild child f. seeks sim.
slim n/s m. 28–35 with GSOH for cosy nights in and fun
nights out – Box 12345' is a language of the emotions that
differs radically from that of Shakespeare, Tennyson or
Wordsworth. The public code of the personal column expresses a language of emotional negotiation: it sets out one's
stall in a swap-shop of intimate transactions and communi-
cates desire across time and space. It declaims the most familiar sentiments to complete and total strangers whilst at
the same time specifying a limited constituency (for example, 'wild', 'slim', 'n/s', 'm.', '28–35', 'GSOH') among them.
At the end of a telephone line is a voice-mail system that
collects any responses to the emotional appeal for later pe-
rusal, ranking, action or disposal. If the personal column
pronounces a desire for intimacy, it does so publicly in the
context of an exercise of choice. Intimacy, here, contrives to
be an exchange relationship: each person offers certain qualities to an audience of strangers and each specifies what quali-

ties are valued in return.

Whilst the personal column exposes a highly visible transformation in the languages of intimacy it is merely a tiny detail of much more extensive changes in the organization of emotional attachments. Intimate relationships, their formation and management are associated with communal norms and socially grounded expectations and obligations. Changes at this level of social organization provide clues to wider changes in those norms, obligations and responsibilities. They hint at more extensive social trends in contemporary society and some of the political problematics that accompany them. These trends include changes in the patterning of relationships; for example, increases in single-parent households, rising divorce rates, the spread of 'contractual' marriages and the tendency to substitute serial monogamy (i.e. moving from one partner to another in sequence) for commitment to a life-long partner, and changes in sexual norms and mores, visible both in the rising number of teenage single parents and in the tendency for many established couples to put off child-bearing in order to pursue careers (the DINKS – Double Income No Kids – syndrome), as well as in a wider acceptance of same-sex relationships. Moreover, many social and taxation policies are grounded in assumptions about particular types of long-term relationship and the norms which govern them. Some contemporary trends have generated alarmist policy responses – the Child Support Agency, intended to secure the financial obligation of absent fathers towards their children; Clause 28 of the 1988 Local Government Act, intended to prevent local government from promoting homosexuality in an equal light with heterosexuality; and even certain dimensions of the 1989 NHS and Community Care Act are all targeted at ameliorating the impacts of changes in intimate relationships and personal behaviours and restoring norms that are contradicted by those very social changes.

For Giddens (1992; 1994), these kinds of change signal disjunctures between established norms and the reality of intimate relationships in contemporary society. In particular, Giddens suggests that one of the most important trends occurring in the present is the 'democratization' of emotions. By this, Giddens is not suggesting either that sexual equality in marriage or cohabitation has been achieved or that intimate relationships today are free of power, violence and manipulation. Rather, he is proposing that, as in my example of the personal column above, there is a tendency for such relationships to depend more on negotiation and open exchange than on traditional expectations, roles and norms. If these latter traditional features of marriage and personal relationships are breaking down, together with the social and political frameworks that once supported them, this process does not leave behind simply a void. There is not, at one instant, a culture of marriage and then, at the next, nothing but trouble: the transformation of intimacy signals positive changes in personal relationships even at the same time as the changes generate difficulties and problems for people and institutions alike. Moreover, the breakdown is not something that is external to the choices made and actions taken by people: decisions to engage in different kinds of relationship rebound on the state policies, the behavioural expectations and the communal networks that are the social contexts and conditions of personal life. Perhaps more clearly than anywhere else, the transformation of intimacy indicates the importance of understanding what each person's motives and desires contribute to the major social transformations of our time.

For Giddens, the motives and desires that permeate what has been understood, common-sensically, as the 'private' sphere stand also at the cusp of the major social changes permeating what has been understood, common-sensically, as the 'public' sphere. The kinds of emotional negotiation that Giddens spies in contemporary personal relationships express a number of important principles that are redefining the wider logics of political action in the contemporary world. In particular, they bring to the fore questions of trust, dialogue and autonomy in both the 'private' and the 'public' domains of life. In other words, they disclose that the pursuit of democracy is a force that is driving changes in personal conduct and interaction as well as in social organization.

Giddens offers several reasons why the process of democratization is central to contemporary public and private life, but the core of his assessment is rooted in the observation that modern society is characterized by a high degree of social reflexivity. In a situation where tradition has lost its hold and no longer guarantees the reliability or trustworthiness of individuals or institutions, each person is faced with a series of open choices about how to live her or his life. Self-actualization, realizing one's own identity through personal and social encounters, precisely because tradition and custom no longer guarantee who we are, is a basic condition of modern social life. It is a condition that promotes personal autonomy from socially embedded expectations and opens up the world to exploration and personal experimentation: we can, to an increasing degree, choose who we are and where. In these circumstances, the process of dialogue becomes increasingly central to the conduct of personal and public life simultaneously. It becomes central to the conduct of personal life because there is no longer any fixed system of roles or norms of behaviour. Where men once expected to inhabit an uninterrupted masculine public world of work, politics and commerce and expected women to dwell apart from their public roles in a private sphere of domestic and nurturing activity, today virtually equal numbers of women and men are found in the labour force. Men often compete with women (although still on privileged terms) for public positions and it appears that women themselves are choosing to abandon marriage in large numbers. For many intimate relationships to work successfully today, there has to be a high degree of dialogue between partners who acknowledge the other's rights, desires and ambitions. Dialogue becomes increasingly important in the public sphere because mass global migration and the world-wide spread of modern media have transformed modern societies into actual or virtual cosmopolitan cultures. The differences thrown up by a cosmopolitan culture can be resolved in one of two ways: through violence or through dialogue.

For Giddens, it is crucial that we grasp the positive potential of contemporary social changes in order to foster the conditions through which violence can be tamed and dialogue expanded. In part, this is why he points to the opportunities contained in modern intimate relationships, because it is in the private and personal sphere that individuals develop a basic framework for handling their desires and feelings. As he writes:

> To the extent that it comes into being, a democracy of the emotions would have major implications for the furtherance of formal public democracy. Individuals who have a good understanding of their own emotional make up, and who are able to communicate effectively on a personal basis, are likely to be well prepared for the wider tasks and responsibilities of citizenship. (1994:16)

People today seek to make things happen through their own, individual actions. In modern society, we are no longer content to leave decisions about the moral qualities of social life to others. We live in a time of neither socialist nor liberal politics but of 'generative politics': a politics that is active at the forefront of the major social questions of environmental change, the quality of life and the role of global institutions. Whether such a politics is expressed through new social movements (what Giddens calls 'life-political' movements – the Greens and feminism being singled out for special mention), through community campaigns for health or housing resources or through alternative economic arrangements (such as local exchange and trading schemes), Giddens suggests the institutions of government must catch up with the processes of democratization that are at the leading edge of contemporary social change. The only way to do this effectively is to transform the institutions of government – including the welfare state – and connected agencies so that individual people can feel confident about placing their trust in organizations that, for far too long, have appeared as self-interested and disconnected from people's everyday concerns. In short, it is necessary for governments to work with, and not against, the social reflexivity of modern society in order to have any hope at all of securing a political consensus on how we should live today.

Concluding comments

Even this brief encounter with Giddens's work will have given some sense of its enormous scope and vigour. Yet it is a project which is far from complete. There is really no indication that either the quantity or intellectual sweep of his writings is about to diminish. Indeed, Giddens's current project is about as strenuous as it can get. The reconnection of academic sociology to the major political questions fac-

ing modern governments, whilst at the same time directing
an institution as unwieldy as the London School of Economics and Political Science, is a task that few serious schol-
ars could undertake. Across the last three decades, Giddens's
scholarship has been central to the redefinition and reconstruction of the intellectual scope of the discipline of sociology. Now, it seems this contribution was a limbering-up
period for tackling the big political questions that suffuse
both the everyday and institutional organization of modern
societies. Anyone who is interested in the ways that political programmes are influenced by public intellectuals and
anyone who is curious about how sociological concepts spi-
ral in and out of everyday life should continue to watch this
space.

References

Beck, U., Lash, S. and Giddens, A. (1994) 'Preface' in U. Beck, S. Lash
    and A. Giddens, *Reflexive Modernization: Politics, Tradition and Aes-
    thetics in the Modern Social Order*, Cambridge: Polity Press, pp. vi–
    viii.
Dawe, A. (1970) 'The Two Sociologies', *British Journal of Sociology*, vol.
    21, pp. 207–18.
Douglas, J. (1967) *The Social Meanings of Suicide*, Princeton, NJ:
    Princeton University Press.
Durkheim, É. (1895) (1982) *The Rules of Sociological Method*, London:
    Macmillan.
Durkheim, É. (1897) (1963) *Suicide: A Sociological Study*, London:
    Routledge.
Giddens, A. (1971) *Capitalism and Modern Social Theory: An Analysis of
    the Writings of Marx, Weber and Durkheim*, Cambridge: Cambridge
    University Press.
Giddens, A. (ed.) (1972a) *Émile Durkheim: Selected Writings*, trans. A.
    Giddens, Cambridge: Cambridge University Press.
Giddens, A. (1972b) *Politics and Sociology in the Thought of Max Weber*,

London: Macmillan.

Giddens, A. (1973) *The Class Structure of the Advanced Societies*, London: Hutchinson.

Giddens, A. (ed.) (1974) *Positivism and Sociology*, London: Heinemann.

Giddens, A. (1976) *New Rules of Sociological Method: A Positive Critique of Interpretative Sociologies*, London: Hutchinson.

Giddens, A. (1977) *Studies in Social and Political Theory*, London: Hutchinson.

Giddens, A. (1979) *Central Problems in Social Theory: Action, Structure and Contradiction in Social Analysis*, Basingstoke: Macmillan.

Giddens, A. (1981) *A Contemporary Critique of Historical Materialism: Volume 1*, second edition 1995, Basingstoke: Macmillan.

Giddens, A. (1984) *The Constitution of Society: Outline of the Theory of Structuration*, Cambridge: Polity Press.

Giddens, A. (1985) *The Nation State and Violence*, Cambridge: Polity Press.

Giddens, A. (1990) *The Consequences of Modernity*, Cambridge: Polity Press.

Giddens, A. (1991) *Modernity and Self-Identity: Self and Society in the Later Modern Age*, Cambridge: Polity Press.

Giddens, A. (1992) *The Transformation of Intimacy*, Cambridge: Polity Press.

Giddens, A. (1994) *Beyond Left and Right: The Future of Radical Politics*, Cambridge: Polity Press.

Giddens, A. (1996) *In Defence of Sociology: Essays, Interpretations and Rejoinders*, Cambridge: Polity Press.

Giddens, A. and Stanworth, P. (eds) (1974) *Élites and Power in British Society*, Cambridge: Cambridge University Press.

Sainsbury, P. (1955) *Suicide in London*, London: Chapman & Hall.

Interview One

Life and Intellectual Career

CHRISTOPHER PIERSON   *In your writings you have often empha-sized the connections between social change and individual iden-tity. Could we start by applying this approach to your own experience? How would you describe your early life and back-ground?*

ANTHONY GIDDENS   I was part of the socially mobile post-war generation. I was born in Edmonton in north London. Ed-monton was, and is, an underprivileged and undistinguished area with few landmarks. Later on my parents moved out to Palmers Green, a slightly more up-market neighbourhood. Until I left to go to university, these regions of north London marked the bounds of my life. We didn't even think of our-selves as living in 'London'; London meant the centre of the city, many miles onwards from where we lived. I was very occasionally taken to see the sights of London by my grandfa-ther, but essentially until my late teens I had hardly ever been to 'London' at all. It was like a foreign city. At the same time, I always felt quite alien from my local surroundings and was desperate to get away. The suburbs of outer London were some-thing of a wasteland and on some level or another anyone living there at that time knew them to be such. Yet it was also a total, enclosed world. I still feel ambivalent towards the neighbourhood I grew up in. I have no direct ties with it any more; I have no relatives there, although I am still in touch with some childhood friends who have continued to live in and around the area all their lives. The area has an instant familiarity for me when I go back, but even now I have a sense of relief on leaving it again. The main reason I do go back, in fact, is to watch the Spurs, which I do whenever they are playing at home. Sport has always been a major part of my life. The part of Edmonton I come from was only about a mile away from the Tottenham ground. In true *Fever Pitch* style I was first taken by my father when I was seven, and started going with a group of friends not too long after that.

Tell me something about your parents. What kind of background were they from?

My father worked for London Transport. He was a clerical worker in an office which dealt with refurbishing the carriages on the underground. For example, he dealt with ordering fabric for the seats. He was frequently outraged about the behaviour of people using the underground. He would tell stories of seats being slashed, covered with paint and ripped out in their entirety. Perhaps he only saw the bad end of it, but according to what he used to say vandalism on the underground was widespread and continuous. I accepted what he said as reality because in a way it conformed to my own experiences. I'm sceptical today of those who claim that crime is spiralling out of control and who look back to an age of social order, when person and property were respected. Some of my earliest memories are of petty crime. When we were only about seven years old, my friends would look for ways of stealing small items from shops, mostly sweets and other goodies like that, which at that time were in short supply. So you see you are speaking to someone who once mixed with criminals! When I was a bit older violence was a commonplace part of our lives. I belonged to an informal boys' gang which wasn't itself a violent one. Many other gangs in the area were inclined to violence and their members went around armed with bicycle chains and knives. We lived in more or less chronic fear of such groups, although the worst that happened to me was that I was occasionally roughed up by them.

And your mother?

She worked all the time, but only in the home. She stopped work, as was normal, soon after she got married. Somehow she changed over the course of her life from being an easy-going and happy young woman to becoming psychologically housebound. When she was younger she was very sociable, but later on she and my father only occasionally went out with friends or invited anyone home. My mother was one of identical twins and this had an enormous impact on her life. The main person she always needed to be near and see often was her twin sister, who married my father's best friend. Most people couldn't tell my mother and her sister apart and they had all the usual experiences of twins. For instance an acquaintance might come up to my mother and say 'You just walked straight past me in the street yesterday.' But of course it was my mother's twin she had seen, who might not have known her at all.

When I started off in academic life I read a lot about twins and I still keep up with the research literature today. The theme of twins, the other who is one's shadow, occurs in a whole variety of guises in literature. The study of twins has a prime place in psychology and the social sciences and large claims about the impact of genetic inheritance on our behaviour are made on the basis of twins studies. The whole thing is very much back in fashion at the moment. My experience of my mother and her twin sister doesn't conform to the new conventional wisdom about the influence of genes on personality. My mother and her sister were almost identical to look at, but their personalities were very different. My aunt was always more bouncy, confident and strong-willed than my mother. In my eyes they developed their respective personalities out of the very closeness of their lifelong interaction. Their characteristics were complementary and that reinforced their mutual dependence.

Do you yourself have brothers and sisters?

I have a brother who is almost ten years younger than me. He is a very successful director of television commercials who now lives in Los Angeles and works in Hollywood. Like me I think he has felt the strong need to escape from his origins, except that he has chosen to move much further away. He spent a considerable period in Hong Kong before moving to the United States and hence hasn't lived in Britain for more than twenty years. He has gone on to the big time.

I did, very briefly, have a sister. My mother gave birth to a girl who only lived for about two weeks. I don't think my mother ever recovered from the child's death. She suffered from recurrent depressions and no doubt this was one of the main factors that produced her later isolation from the wider world.

What about your own educational background?

I passed the 11-plus exam and went to the local grammar school. How I passed, I have no idea. We had almost no preparation for it and I had only the foggiest of notions about what it was; I didn't think of it as anything important at all. But it did have consequences running through my whole life. The grammar schools were so separate and different from the secondary modern schools. My brother didn't pass the 11-plus and even today I'm not sure he has got over the feelings of rejection that this produced. The secondary moderns were like another world, completely removed from that of the grammar schools. I had no particular interest in school work and was hardly a model pupil or star performer academically. I did develop intellectual interests, but these were ones opposed to the orthodox school values. I started reading books off the syllabus in philosophy, psychology and anthropology – more as a protest gesture than anything else, because I really had very little knowledge of what these subjects were about. I never really liked the atmosphere of the school, which was quite a rigid disciplinary institution. I learned some sort of respect for academic achievement there, but expressed it more by distancing myself from what one was supposed to know or learn about. I didn't get any of this from my home environment, since neither of my parents read very widely and there were very few books in the home.

No one in my family before me had been to college or had any connection with higher education. How I got to university is a prime example of how much one's life is influenced by contingency, although I suppose there was a bit of determination there too. I thought I would try for university, but I got little or no help from the school because I was thought of as only a very mediocre student. I went to the local library and looked through a list of universities in a handbook. London, Oxford and Cambridge were beyond the pale – I never even considered them. I opted for places I thought might at least take some interest in me. So I applied to Nottingham,

Reading and Hull. I was rejected out of hand by the first two. However, Hull at that time was experimenting with interviewing a diversity of people, even those who had not particularly good qualifications. I was interviewed and accepted there, something again which in retrospect seems like one of life's little mysteries. I went to Hull to do philosophy and perhaps the interviewer was impressed by the fact that I had actually read some.

As it turned out I wasn't in fact able to pursue a degree in the subject. The philosophy department in Hull was very small and the main lecturer was away for the year. So I was pushed off to look for another subject to study. I was moved over to the psychology department but was told I would have to study psychology alongside sociology. I had no idea at all what sociology was about. But I was very lucky. Peter Worsley, who later moved on to become professor of sociology at Manchester, was teaching sociology at Hull. He was something of an inspirational figure, already well published, lively and politically engaged. Out of perversity I was the only one in my cohort of students who wasn't a member of the Socialist Society. Everyone else, like Peter himself, sported socialist badges of some sort. I was sympathetic to these political views, but was much more impressed with Worsley's intellectual qualities and the range of his academic knowledge. Worsley is an anthropologist as well as a sociologist and he always taught in a strongly comparative way, drawing in examples from societies of all kinds. Under his influence, once I got some sense of what the subject seemed to be about, I turned much more to sociology than psychology. However, this academic cosmopolitanism was good for me. I still try to read quite widely in psychology and anthropology and I've never thought of academic divisions in the aggressively territorial way some people do.

When I arrived there, Hull was for me a completely new terrain. I had never been to the north of England before. Hull wasn't a place which nurtured the Industrial Revolution, but many other towns and villages I got to know in Yorkshire were. The first time I saw the serried ranks of back-to-back workers' cottages stretching up and down the hills it was a revelation. The industrial villages to me were as exotic as any of the other more flamboyantly different places I've since visited around the world. I have no doubt that this influenced the views I later developed in sociology. I was deeply impressed by the strangeness and the enveloping nature of what I saw as the visible form of the Industrial Revolution.

Hull itself was different. It was still a fishing town, although the industry was already in quite steep decline. I really enjoyed the city. Active ports have a liveliness all of their own. We often used to go down to the pubs where the fishermen went for their entertainment. Like the Yorkshire miners, the fishermen were a prime example of an occupational community. Fishing was as rough and tough as mining, and full of the same rituals. People who work in hazardous occupations have a variety of charms and superstitions which tend to form an important part of their lives. The fishermen had many beliefs and practices that seemed straight out of the anthropology texts which Peter Worsley quoted. Fishing was also a strongly communal way of life. The boats competed with one another for their catches yet they had a strong sense of solidarity.

Fishermen might be at sea for quite a long while. Fishermen's wives tended to be robustly independent since in effect they were bringing up their families on their own. Fathers played very little part in caring for children. When they weren't away, most of the men spent their evenings out in each other's company. It seems to me that the idea that there were once much stronger forms of fathering than there are now is largely a myth. My own father was as 'absent' as any other – since he had to travel an hour and a half to get to work, he left early and came back quite late in the evenings.

What happened after Hull?

I went off to do a further degree at the London School of Economics. It was a characteristically muddled decision. I knew very little about the LSE. I had by that time acquired some academic ambitions, but initially focused my sights on Manchester or Oxford. Peter Worsley suggested the LSE and I took his advice. I didn't register for a PhD at the LSE but did a Master's course. I had no real thought of pursuing an academic career. I was thinking of trying to go into the Civil Service and the LSE seemed to be the right sort of place to prepare for that. The Master's course I followed was mainly based upon a thesis and I in fact ended up writing a dissertation equivalent in length to a PhD. I have to confess that I didn't take it all too seriously so I wrote about a fun topic. The title was 'Sport and Society in Contemporary England'. I took it on tongue in cheek but it actually proved intriguing. I looked primarily at the development of sport in nineteenth-century England. England was the home of the Industrial Revolution and of the changes I later associated more generally with modernity. It was also the place where many of the sports which have since become popular across the world originated.

I thought there was more than an accidental connection between these. Most modern sport is essentially a creation of the nineteenth and early twentieth centuries. The history of soccer, rugby, cricket, tennis and other sports goes back much earlier, but not until the nineteenth century did these sports take on the form they still have today. I tried to show that sport became rationalized, using the notion drawn from Max Weber. Sports acquired rules and regulations, as well as fixed playing locales, which by and large none of them had before – they were much more rough and ready. Some games, like lawn tennis, were effectively invented by individuals. Real tennis or court tennis had been played for centuries, but a certain Major Wingfield was the first to draw up rules for the new game of lawn tennis, which swiftly became just 'tennis'.

I also tried to relate the development of sport and leisure to class divisions. Working-class sports tended to be intensely competitive and professionalized. Middle-class sports, on the other hand, were permeated by the ethos of the amateur and down-played competitiveness: rugby union, for instance, didn't have leagues. I argued that these different orientations to sport reflected contrasting forms of work situation. Working-class jobs offered no chance of career advancement; the only way working-class people could get on was through cooperation and collective trade union pressure. In sport, as a reaction, they looked for a fierce competitive individualism. Middle-class work careers are based precisely upon individualistic competition; outside work, middle-class sport hence placed an emphasis upon collegiality and collaboration. In studying sport I was again drawn to the theme of ritual. Sport is for many people the last residue of passion in the old religious sense and all sports events are ceremonials.

What was your early experience of the LSE? Does it seem strange to be back there now as its Director?

I was in the sociology department at the School. During my first year I was supervised by David Lockwood, who was just making a name for himself in sociology. Lockwood had worked very closely with Ralf Dahrendorf. In fact they ran a celebrated 'evening seminar' at the LSE, some while before I arrived there, which Dahrendorf refers to in the dedication of his famous book *Class and Class Conflict in Industrial Society*. Dahrendorf had written a PhD while at the LSE on the topic of 'the unskilled worker'. Even at that date Dahrendorf was already a legendary figure. Stories abounded about how quickly he had written the dissertation and what an extraordinary capacity he had for work, coupled to a highly original cast of mind. Lockwood himself had written a celebrated book on the middle class, *The Black Coated Worker*. He wanted me to pursue similar issues and he took a dim view when I fixed on the sociology of sport. In my second year at the LSE I was supervised by Asher Tropp, who worked mainly on the sociology of the professions, in particular the teaching profession. Both Lockwood and Tropp were supportive, but neither took me all that seriously – unsurprisingly, because I had quite self-consciously adopted a 'playful' topic.

I did complete the dissertation but I didn't find the LSE a particularly welcoming environment. I missed out on a lot. I never took full advantage of the array of intellectual figures of world repute who were there. Only afterwards did I discover the full riches of the LSE, when I set out to read Popper, Oakeshott, Marshall and others. Even the professors were frighteningly remote figures in those days, let alone the Director, whom I don't believe I ever even caught sight of. The LSE was wasted on me and I want to do my best to make sure this doesn't happen to others now. A college in the centre of a large city is necessarily a place where people are coming and going all the time. A special effort has to be made to make such an environment welcoming to students, who after all come to the LSE from a much greater diversity of backgrounds than would be true of any other university institution.

You obviously didn't become a civil servant: how did you come to get started in an academic career?

Like many of the major things in life this happened in quite a casual way. The big decisions one takes almost without thinking about them, whereas one agonizes over minor dilemmas. I was still planning to go into the Civil Service, but Tropp pointed out a job which had been advertised in sociology teaching at the University of Leicester. He suggested I might have a chance and without giving it much thought I applied. I wasn't really planning to go even if I should get the job but wanted the experience of the interview.

The interview itself, or rather the informal meeting prior to the formal interview, changed my mind. The informal meeting was with two very interesting gentlemen, neither of whom I had heard about before, both sporting quite heavy Central European accents. They launched straight away into a discussion of the sociology of sport, which, unlike anyone at the LSE, and also to some degree unlike myself, they actually seemed to take seriously. In fact they talked about it much more interestingly than I was able to do and much of the so-called informal interview consisted of a dialogue between them with me as an interested listener.

One was Ilya Neustadt, who was the head of the department at Leicester and had built up a department which for a while was probably the leading centre in the country. The other was Norbert Elias. Both had spent some while at the LSE, but neither was able to obtain a permanent teaching position there. Norbert Elias had only a junior position at Leicester. When I first went there he was completely unknown in the English-speaking world. His now-renowned book *The Civilizing Process* had not been translated. It hadn't even been widely available in Germany. It first appeared, I believe, in 1939, not the most auspicious date for a work on the progress of civilization.

Unknown though he might have been, Norbert acted as though he were a world-famous scholar – as he was indeed to become. He taught me the value of dedication and perseverance. If you are relatively untalented, as I am, you can make up a good deal of the difference simply by giving more time to your chosen endeavour than others do and sticking with it through the difficult patches. Paul Getty said, 'My formula for success is rise early, work late, and strike oil.' In other words, the Puritan ethic isn't enough – you need some luck along the way. Having Norbert as an example to follow was my luck at the time. I struck oil, metaphorically at least, at Leicester.

Norbert worked harder than anyone else in the university. He also possessed an encyclopedic knowledge of culture – he was sociologist, historian, anthropologist and theorist of law. He wasn't quite Max Weber incarnate, but to my mind he came pretty close. Norbert's ideas influenced me a lot although I only realized this in retrospect. I was never persuaded about the central themes of *The Civilizing Process* or the quasi-Freudian theory of repression which underlay it. On the other hand Norbert to me quite rightly stressed the significance of developmental processes and the open, contingent nature of social life.

What made the sociology department at Leicester so distinctive?

It was partly the insistence upon a comparative and developmental perspective which Neustadt and Elias shared. Sociology at Leicester was quite different from the Fabian traditions of thought, closely UK-oriented, which tended to predominate at the LSE. Leicester attracted and also produced a large number of younger sociologists, most of whom were committed to initiating what was then a new subject – outside of a few universities where the discipline had longer traditions. Neustadt and Elias both allocated a significant role for social theory and saw this as stretching well beyond the confines of sociology itself – a view which I also hold. There were plenty of very competent technical researchers at Leicester in those days, but the department never became dominated wholly by one or the other. Consequently there were continuous and lively debates.

It was really only at this point that I committed myself to an academic career, and started to pursue the interests which have preoccupied me ever since. I began to explore theoretical issues ranging across the social sciences, and took up reading philosophy again too. I came to see sociology as methodologically challenging in a peculiarly interesting way. You know the old joke: 'Sociology is the study of people who don't need to be studied by people who do.' I took, and still do take, the implied criticism seriously. Rather than making sociology and the rest of the social sciences redundant, we should see that social science stands in a reflexive relation to its subject-matter, human social action.

Why did you move on from Leicester?

I got the opportunity to spend two years in North America. I went first of all to Simon Fraser University in Vancouver and later to the University of California, Los Angeles. These were very formative experiences for me. In Vancouver the university was seething with discontent. One of my closest colleagues had been a leading figure in the Free Speech Movement in Berkeley. Meeting him and some other people around him was my first taste of North American populist radicalism. In Europe we were used to people calling themselves 'radicals', but for the most part they lived ordinary lives outside of their political activities. The North American radicals at that point were very much more venturesome. For them radicalism had to include every aspect of lifestyle. The well-known sociologist Tom Bottomore was there as chairman of the department. Tom was a European-style radical: he held quite left-wing beliefs, but he lived a perfectly ordinary bourgeois lifestyle. He had terrible clashes with the others because they thought his attitudes were hypocritical.

I spent nine months in Vancouver and about eighteen months in Los Angeles. I was teaching at UCLA during the key year of 1968 to 1969. What was going on there made the political confrontations in Britain seem pretty small beer. The first afternoon I got to Los Angeles I went down for a walk along the beach. I thought it would be deserted but it was full of people, an utterly amazing scene. No one in Europe then had heard of hippies. But in California alternative lifestyle movements were already proliferating. The beach looked something like the fall of the Roman Empire. It was a maze of gaudy colours. People were dressed like characters from a biblical scene, or so it seemed for someone who'd not encountered the hippies before. Ranged alongside the beach was the full panoply of state power: a long fleet of police cars, several with shot-guns protruding through the open windows.

A whole variety of movements developed, including the large-scale movement against the Vietnam war. It was a time of great social experimentation. I had one colleague whom I got to know quite well very shortly after I arrived in Los Angeles. He was primarily a mathematician. He was also the most conventional person one could imagine, or so it appeared. He was everybody's idea of the four-square American. At one point I didn't see him for a period of some three months. I was walking across the campus one day when I saw a gaunt, Jesus-looking figure, with long hair and a beard, coming towards me. I didn't recognize him until he stopped to say hello. It was my colleague the mathematician. He had left his family, left the university and moved to the desert in New Mexico to drop out and live on a commune. He wasn't unusual. Years later I had a letter from him. He was trying to get back into academic life. Naturally enough he wasn't having much success because by then he'd been out of the academic community for fifteen years.

For many observers the movements of the 1960s disappeared as quickly as they came, and either they had no long-term influence or their impact – as many right-wing commentators now say – was a destructive one. I don't agree with these views. There was a lot of craziness around, but the ideas and themes of the 1960s movements have had a profound effect. They helped introduce a fluidity to lifestyles which has not gone away; they established some of the moral and political impulses which, while originally largely regarded as eccentric, have become part of the mainstream – including a stress on personal autonomy, the emancipation of women, ecological issues and the push for universal human rights. Some sectors of the peace movement foresaw the end of war, a view then commonly regarded as absurd. They were, however, prescient: we live in a world in which there is at least a good chance that traditional large-scale war between nation-states is disappearing. These movements used the rhetoric of Marxism, but they were universally anti-Communist. *Obsolete Communism* was after all the title of one of the best-known texts of the period, written by the student activist Daniel Cohn-Bendit: the phrase has now become a reality, even if the dissolution of Communism occurred in quite a different way to that which Cohn-Bendit predicted. It is entirely possible that we will see a new flowering of counter-cultural social movements again at some point in the relatively near future. We appear on the face of things to live in a society with no alternatives, and in spite of the existence of Soviet-style societies this was also the common-sense view in Western countries in the 1950s and early 1960s. I don't feel we are yet at the end of history.

How did your period in North America influence your writings?

During the period I was in North America I only wrote a few articles. I did do one or two commentaries on the social movements, particularly the anti-war movement, for European papers and periodicals. In spite of, or perhaps as a reaction to, the exciting events going on I was beginning to work on fairly abstract questions of social theory and the origins of classical social thought. The reading I did for this in Los Angeles formed the basis of the first book I wrote, *Capitalism and Modern Social Theory*. I also gave a course at UCLA which covered the three main thinkers who appeared in the book. I had quite a few hostile reactions from conservatives because of lecturing about Marx. No one ever disrupted my classes, though – as happened to other teachers on the campus.

So then you came back to England?

I came back, but over the next few years I often returned to California. As a consequence when you add it all up I've spent a significant proportion of my life there. Even today, though there are very strong elements of social conservatism, California is in many ways more experimental on the level of everyday life than Europe.

After I returned, I wanted to move on from Leicester and it was at this point that I went to Cambridge. I replaced John

Goldthorpe, who had achieved an international reputation for himself by co-authoring *The Affluent Worker* studies, together with David Lockwood and two other colleagues. Goldthorpe moved to Nuffield College, Oxford, where he still is today. I stepped into his shoes, largely through his good auspices, because not only did I take over his lectureship but I followed him as a fellow of King's. Like Goldthorpe I taught first of all in the economics faculty, of which I was a member for quite a few years. Sociology wasn't at that time at all well established in Cambridge, nor was political science. At about the time I came to Cambridge, the teaching of social sciences was for the first time grouped under the control of a committee, the Social and Political Sciences Committee. But this had no faculty status.

What were your attitudes to Cambridge? It must have had a different culture from Leicester – it must also have been very different from the University of California.

Certainly it was different from both. I found it a hard process of adjustment, although from the beginning I appreciated the generous provision of time and resources there is at Cambridge. I feel I was productive throughout most of the long period I spent there. In the early 1970s, for example, besides *Capitalism and Modern Social Theory* I wrote *The Class Structure of the Advanced Societies*, a study of Max Weber's political writings, I translated and edited a book of selections from Durkheim and wrote a methodological book with a Durkheimian-style title, *New Rules of Sociological Method*.

By this time I had got an overall project which was to occupy me for a long while and which I am still in effect working on today. I wanted to do three things: offer a reinterpretation of the history of social thought, particularly in the nineteenth and early twentieth centuries; develop a reconstruction of the logic and method of the social sciences; and produce an analysis of the emergence of modern institutions.

You said you had trouble adjusting to Cambridge. Could you expand on this a little?

Cambridge was largely dominated by people from Oxbridge backgrounds. The large majority had got at least one degree at Oxbridge, whether undergraduate or graduate. There weren't many people like me who came completely from the outside. So I had no preparatory socialization at all. I was working on issues of elites and power in the early 1970s. It struck me what an extraordinary continuity there must have been, especially in previous generations, for those who went to public schools, moved on to Oxbridge and from there went into government, the foreign service, law or the other older professions. The buildings of the top public schools look very similar to Oxbridge colleges, which in turn resemble the various other corridors of power. Even some of the details were similar. In Cambridge colleges, the name of each fellow is handwritten on a board by the entry to the college staircases. The same is true in the public schools and places like the Inns of Court. One could almost suppose it was a single sign writer covering all these institutions.

Moreover, there was, and is, nothing like the college system in universities outside Oxbridge. Also I had to fight battles by the very fact of teaching sociology, which was widely regarded as simultaneously uninteresting and dangerous. Sociology had no effective institutional home. It functioned well enough, in a limited way, within the economics faculty but was limited only to a few courses.

During your relatively early years in Cambridge you started writing quite widely about Continental social thought; not just the classical writers, but current trends in Continental social philosophy and social theory. How did this come about?

It had its roots further back. Before I spent the period in North America I studied for two summer vacations in Paris, working in the Bibliothèque Nationale. I also spent a period of time learning to read German, with a view to studying texts of Marx and Max Weber in the original. I wasn't only reading these authors themselves, I was reading commentaries about them in French and German. Through some of those commentators, such as the French sociologist Raymond Aron, I broadened out to a variety of other contemporary authors. I started reading in the tradition of hermeneutics – a tradition to which Max Weber was affiliated. I read widely in the literature of Marxism and also philosophers such as Husserl and Heidegger. I came back to them again a few years subsequently, around about the mid to late 1970s. I was trying to work out how these various strands of thought might relate to the ideas then current in the English-speaking world. Sociology then was still largely dominated by American authors. Robert K. Merton and Talcott Parsons remain the most quoted authors. Like many others, including their critics from the scene of the new social movements, I sought to define myself by using them as a critical foil. I drew quite widely upon Continental thought to do so.

You were one of the co-founders of Polity Press in 1984. What made you decide to initiate this venture? Were you thinking at that time of moving outside of academic life altogether?

No, I never considered such a course of action. Whatever my difficulties in Cambridge, I have always felt happy in academic life and particularly being in regular contact with students. The celebrated French social theorist Michel Foucault towards the end of his life was asked how he would characterize himself and he simply said 'a teacher'. That's how I see myself too. Teaching, especially the giving of lectures to so many different student audiences, has been one of the great and enduring pleasures of my life.

We founded Polity for several reasons. My co-founders were David Held, now professor of politics at the Open University, and John Thompson, who is reader in sociology and a fellow of Jesus College, Cambridge. David and I were already series editors for other publishers. As such an editor, however, one doesn't get much control over a list. We thought rather than work for other publishers we might as well see if we could work for ourselves by establishing our own imprint. We also wanted to make an intervention of a political and cultural kind. One of the objects of Polity since the beginning has been to mediate between Anglo-Saxon and Continental thought, the same sort of thing as I was trying to achieve individually in my own books. A bit presumptuously, we thought we could do a better job than established academic publishers, who had to send out manuscripts for assessments by academics before forming a judgement about them. Since we could read and assess the manuscripts directly, we were in a position to make much quicker decisions, and I hope more informed decisions, than an orthodox publisher would be.

Polity has since become one of the best-known publishers in the social sciences and humanities world-wide. But how did you get it off the ground in the first place?

We contacted several publishers to see if they might be interested in forming a joint enterprise with us, into which they would put financial capital and we would put the intellectual capital. The firm we were most interested in, and was most interested in us, was Blackwell. Blackwell put up the funding for a joint venture. Polity Press is a separate company, linked to Blackwell by a joint holding company. We feel that Polity has achieved a good deal of what we set out to do. We publish some seventy to eighty titles a year. We've done a lot of translations from the major European languages and Polity is particularly strong in the areas of social, political and cultural theory.

Polity was founded at about the same time that you were appointed to the chair of sociology in Cambridge?

I was appointed to the chair in 1987. It was an important transition point for me, because it gave me considerably more influence inside the university. I was pleased and relieved to get the chair. Over the preceding period of some ten years I was rejected on nine occasions for promotion to a readership. I think this was a record until it was broken by somebody else quite recently. As a result of my appointment to the chair I was able to develop support for creating a better institutional framework for social science in Cambridge. The social and political sciences faculty was set up in 1988. So far as I know, it was the first new faculty to be established in Cambridge for more than half a century, and it took quite a lot of diplomatic wangling to get it through.

You moved to become Director of the LSE very early in 1997. Why did you decide to leave Cambridge after being there for so long?

I don't think there is any other job in academic life I would in fact have left for. Even if I wasn't completely happy while I was a student at the School, as I mentioned before, I long since came to recognize its extraordinary qualities and the importance of its place not just in intellectual but in political and economic life. I had no second thoughts about leaving Cambridge at all.

What would you like to achieve for the LSE?

I'd like to help propel the LSE towards another golden age, and I'd like to ensure that the School has a concrete impact upon the world. The LSE has existed for more than a century and was conceived of by Sidney and Beatrice Webb as an institution which would contribute in a practical way to the betterment of the world. It has a consistent history of doing so and, contrary to what many may think, it has never been a partisan institution. Since its beginnings it has had a mix of thinkers from the left and right. Following World War II, the LSE has had an impact on two successive phases of social and political change. The LSE was the place where some of the basic ideas and policies about the post-war welfare state were elaborated. Clement Attlee once taught at the School, while of course William Beveridge was for a while its Director. On a more intellectual level, figures such as Tawney, Titmuss and Marshall took the lead.

The LSE was the site of some of the dialogues and battles surrounding the new social movements in the late 1960s and early 1970s. What is less generally recognized is that the LSE was also the source of some of the key thinking and policy-making which went into the political 'counter-revolution' with the rise of Thatcherism. Margaret Thatcher's favourite economic philosopher, Friedrich von Hayek, taught at the School. As I would see it, we are now in a third phase and the LSE should play a fundamental role in elaborating responses to the new world in which we find ourselves. I don't mean this in only a political sense. As we will go on to discuss later, we're living through a period of intense social, political and economic change. It is one which demands new responses all the way through from politics to business and everyday life. I would like to see the LSE as a centre of dialogue and debate, as well as a research centre, relevant to a diagnosis of our times.

What about the future of the universities in general? What does the future actually hold for universities, especially in the light of the rise of new information technologies?

The position of universities has shifted, as has the role of intellectuals. When I started out, teaching in a university was widely regarded as one of the most prestigious things one could do. This hardly remains true today. There are several reasons. One is the massive expansion of higher education, which means that the status of professor is not as distinctive as it used to be. Another is the increasing prestige attached to occupations in business, the City and media. Universities simply aren't regarded in the same light as they used to be. A further factor is that universities now have to compete with a wider range of knowledge-producers than before. Competitors include think-tanks, research agencies, survey agencies, management consultancies and media companies.

The longer-term impact of information technology is still imponderable – as it is in the sphere of publishing too. Information technology of course expands the range of available research materials and has already substantially changed the working patterns of students. The new generation is unable to work without computers. On the other hand, I think a good deal of the current speculation about information technology is misplaced. Electronic communication doesn't replace the need to be with others, in a circumscribed place. Consider the example of the City itself. It is one of the main hubs of the new global electronic economy. At the same time it is a physical place, concentrated within a square mile. With the advent of the new technologies, academics and business people go to more conferences rather than less. You still need to look into the eyes of the other. The same applies in universities. Some aspects of established universities undoubtedly will change. On the other hand, their appeal is likely to be enhanced rather than undermined by the new technologies. This is, as the sociologists Deirdre Boden and Harvey Molotch say, 'the compulsion of proximity'.

One final point: could I ask you to say just a bit more about the driving motives of your intellectual career? You seem to describe your life as a rather haphazard affair, but to me your intellectual activities have always had a highly focused and determined character.

The continuity in my intellectual career has been what held much of the rest of my life together. I didn't aim to be an academic, but once I had launched into it, I found intellectual activity wholly absorbing. I've been doggedly pursuing the same project since the beginning. I wanted to take a fresh look at the past development of classical social thought; develop a new methodological framework for the social sciences; and analyse the distinctive qualities of modernity. There's more than enough to keep anyone busy in all that.

Interview Two

The Sociological Classics and Beyond

CHRISTOPHER PIERSON *Perhaps we could begin not quite at the beginning but with* Capitalism and Modern Social Theory, *which was first published in 1971. This critical exegesis of the work of Marx, Durkheim and Weber has been a lifeline to generations of undergraduate students. In the preface, you described these three writers as the outstanding figures in establishing the principal frame of reference of modern sociology. Tell us something about the context in which you set out to write about them.*

ANTHONY GIDDENS At the time I wrote *Capitalism and Modern Social Theory*, Talcott Parsons was the most significant figure interpreting the history of social thought. Famously, in *The Structure of Social Action*, his main book, there was hardly any mention of Marx and no original text of Marx was actually quoted. Parsons had a distinctive view of the emergence of sociology in particular and of the development of social theory more widely. This was that there were two developmental phases in the nineteenth and early twentieth centuries. The period up until the 1880s was dominated by the precursors of sociology, such as Comte and Marx. After this came a generation which produced a new and properly sociological synthesis. This idea was very influential at that time. There was often a separation between Marxists, who tended to look only to Marx, and other sociologists, who looked mainly to Durkheim and Weber.

I sought to bring the three together and to treat them in an equivalent way within one volume. Later it became much more conventional to speak of Marx, Durkheim and Weber as 'the three classical founders of sociology'. But when I wrote the book, it wasn't that way. I wrote it partly to counteract, on the one hand, those writers who held that Marx is everything and that Marxism has in some sense revealed the truth of things, whereas the 'bourgeois sociologists' can be ignored; and, on the other hand, the Parsonian view that Marx belonged to an earlier phase in the development of social theory which essentially had been superseded by Durkheim and Weber. I also wanted to give more historical context to the emergence of the ideas of each of these thinkers.

I would like to explore your views on the continuing significance of these founding figures. We might begin with Durkheim. For some commentators, Durkheim is associated above all with ideas such as positivism, the belief that social science could emulate the methods and predictive capacity of the natural sciences, and functionalism, the belief that social institutions can be explained by the functions they perform in the reproduction of society. With a few exceptions these are now seen as the kinds of naive claim that every sophisticated sociologist wants to avoid. Is this a fair judgement on Durkheim's heritage?

Well, I think you probably need to historicize this as well. Here again, Parsons's interpretation was quite important, because it established a certain thematic for what Durkheim's writings were and his main objectives. One should remember that at that time, twenty-five years ago, Durkheim's work was not all that well known by Anglo-Saxon sociologists. Whilst most of the key books were translated, certain of the more interesting and really quite important ones weren't. For example, some of the material from the book that was called *Leçons de sociologie* in French (subsequently translated as *Professional Ethics and Civic Morals*), some of the work on moral education and papers from the *Année Sociologique* were translated later. So the level of scholarship on Durkheim wasn't that high until the British social theorist Steven Lukes wrote what is, I suppose, still the definitive interpretation of Durkheim following on from the Parsonian one.

Parsons held that Durkheim started out from a positivist view and then gradually extricated himself from it and moved towards Weber and Pareto, the other writers that he discussed in *The Structure of Social Action*. I never really thought that view was convincing. I argued, and would still argue, that like any major thinker Durkheim had a number of strands in his writing. He never really managed to integrate these effectively. In the early stages of his writings, there was his discussion of 'treating social facts as things' and, of course, his exposition of functionalism in *The Rules of Sociological Method*. But if one goes back to Durkheim's earliest review articles, his very early writings, he is already there analysing moral consciousness. He is talking about something like spirituality, he is talking about moral ethics. These things seem to have been there from the beginning. He was, from the beginning, a more complex writer than those who see him as a 'functionalist' or 'positivist' allow. He was always struggling to reconcile these differing views. On the one hand, he wanted to treat human social life in a systematic and rigorous way and to that extent his approach is rather like Comte's positive philosophy, seeking to produce something like a positive science of society. On the other hand, from his earliest works, Durkheim always seems to have been clear that human consciousness, morality, spirituality are nothing like events in nature, and whilst we might be able to apply a similar logic and method to human behaviour, the actual subject-matter is plainly very different. I don't think he was ever in any crude sense a positivist, if that means that the natural and social sciences are in some sense the same or that you don't have to recognize the differences. He started out writing about religion and returned to that later on in his life. Religion could hardly be regarded as a 'force of nature', given its preoccupation with the ethical and spiritual.

What I was trying to do in *Capitalism and Modern Social Theory* was to place Durkheim's writing against the backdrop of the development of modern society. Most of the other people who wrote about him didn't really do that. I was particularly interested in his analysis of the rise of modern individualism, its relationship to inequality, the issue of solidarity and the transition between two forms of solidarity. All those questions are still relevant today. If you think of communitarianism and the writings of its leading advocate Amitai Etzioni, for example, these reproduce Durkheimian themes: a condition of freedom and individual self-development is having a community or society that allows for those qualities to be created. They are not just given in the human condition. Durkheim argued that social cohesion is made problematic by the rise of individualism – very much the issue being discussed again now under the banner of communitarianism. On some of these issues, Durkheim's writings still look quite fresh.

Is Durkheim influential in these contemporary debates or is there just some sort of parallel between the two?

Well, he is not as influential as he should be. The debate about communitarianism has been led from two sources. One is the philosophical discussion of liberalism in the hands of Charles Taylor and others. The other is the more policy-oriented agenda set by Etzioni. Durkheim hasn't been referred to much by either group. The one person who you could say has linked up these issues is Dennis Wrong in his book *The Problem of Order*.

What else is of lasting interest in Durkheim's work?

Durkheim had a provocative theory of the transition between premodern and modern society, coupled to an interpretation of modernity itself. Durkheim's contrast between mechanical and organic solidarity is far from exhausted – it is essentially a theory of increasing social complexity. He also developed a theory of inequality linked to it. Traditional societies do create inequalities but these needn't destroy social cohesion if they are controlled (he was in favour of sweeping inheritance taxes) and if there are high levels of social mobility. Given the collapse of Marxism, these ideas are again in fashion.

Are there other areas where you think Durkheim has proved more impressive than the others?

A very important theme in Durkheim is moral individualism, which relates to communitarianism and other current discussions in relation to the family. Durkheim had a particular conception of the nature of modern morality. There must be a moral order for a society to exist at all, but traditional morality can't really be the social glue that holds together modern society – older ideas of community become obsolete. In so far as people now are again arguing about the traditional family and the recovery of community, one could say they are making a category mistake. We can't recapture community or the traditional family in a society with a highly complex division of labour marked by a high degree of individualism. We need some other kind of moral framework, which Durkheim claimed to find in the ethics of the French Revolution. We can have a morality that is both social, in a certain sense collective, but that also recognizes the key significance of individual freedom.

Isn't it true, though, that a lot of these debates now are canvassed with a scepticism towards any kind of moral authority and that this scepticism isn't really there in the same way in the Durkheimian account?

No, the strongest tendency at the moment is to argue that societies have become demoralized. That's the claim of Gertrude Himmelfarb and the view of others on the right. It is also, in a certain sense, Etzioni's view. We are suffering from 'disorders of freedom', in which there are too many rights and not enough obligations around. Whatever one makes of that, it is quite similar to the debate around the turn of the century in which Durkheim was the central figure.

I'm just wondering if in the context of Durkheim, there wasn't actually less scepticism about the capacity to put some kind of moral order in place. Whatever were the problems that modern forms of individualism generated, Durkheim does seem to have had some confidence that a kind of moral order could be generated socially. A lot of commentators now seem much more sceptical that's actually possible at all.

Durkheim envisaged a secular republican state which would recognize both the central significance of human rights and individual freedoms, but at the same time would have a fairly strong measure of solidarity. He thought these were complementary. There are certainly people now who doubt that. I would say the communitarians doubt it: that is, they question what you might call a procedural model of democracy and they want the state to legislate more directly upon the family and other moral issues. They wouldn't accept Durkheim's position, even though there are clear links between what Durkheim says and communitarian views – as in the communitarian critique of free-market philosophies. Durkheim contested the idea that markets can do everything. Marx did too, in a different way. Few thought that this issue would make such a comeback, or that it would be so important at the end of the twentieth century. Indeed some think we have effectively moved back to a world like that of the late nineteenth century, with a return to a market society (although that isn't my view).

Perhaps we could move on to talk about Max Weber? Of the three figures you discussed in Capitalism and Modern Social Theory, *Max Weber is perhaps the one whose reputation seems most secure. His methodology seems to recognize differences between explanation in the natural and social sciences. He seemed to have focused on processes of rationalization and bureaucracy which are crucial to modernity. He appeared to have recognized the centrality of power and the potential for violence. He was pessimistic, not least about the prospects for socialism. I have a couple of questions. First, what do you see as Weber's most enduring contribution to twentieth-century sociology?*

With Weber again one needs to start by understanding the context of his work. Weber was trying to accomplish something rather similar to Durkheim in terms of overall strategy and in relation to politics, but in a very different national context. Durkheim was trying to provide a sociological defence of liberalism. Weber sought to do something similar, but in a context and in a country where liberalism was weak and where there was only a small middle class. His quest for a sociological defence of liberalism turned out to be quite distinct from that of Durkheim. Yet both were trying to show what were the conditions for the success of a liberal democratic state in countries where that state was still in process of formation. Weber was as much preoccupied with the relationship between individualism and collective power as was Durkheim, but he had a different take on those issues. He had a contrasting definition of the state. States for Weber depend on power and territory. There is much more of a Nietzschean thread in this than there is in anything Durkheim has to say. Durkheim saw democracy mainly in moral terms, whereas for Weber it concerns the mobilizing and containment of power.

As to Weber's most enduring contribution, it is bound up with the comparative study of civilizations. Weber was probably the first major thinker to break away from the Eurocentric view of the world, which Marx still largely had. Weber was the first to try to see Western civilization as only one civilization among others, to grasp the clash of civilizations as fundamental to overall world history. Now you have Huntington saying somewhat similar things. I am not endorsing Huntington's view, but that kind of global perspective on different paths of development in different cultural civilizations is just as significant now as it was then.

In political science, Weber is often recognized as a formative figure because of what he has to say primarily about the state but also about the character of power and violence. You have sometimes suggested that, characteristically, sociologists have tended to ignore issues like these.

Weber was a political thinker, economic historian and theorist of jurisprudence. He wasn't only a sociologist; he only
came to sociology pretty reluctantly and only started using
the term quite late in his career. Originally he identified it
with people he disliked, like Schäffle and Comte, thinkers
whom Weber discounted (although Durkheim admired).
When his works were first translated into English, Weber was
regarded primarily as an economist or an economic historian.
Certainly that is how he was seen by Tawney, or by Frank
Knight, who translated Weber's *General Economic History*.

*The other issue I wanted to raise is whether you believe that 'we
are all Weberians now'. Is the discipline of sociology one which is
now principally grounded in ideas that derive from Weber rather
than from the influence of, say, Durkheim or Marx?*

No, I wouldn't say so. Weber had a particular view of things
which I don't think has remained all that persuasive. As I say,
he wasn't primarily a sociologist and he refused the kind of
theoretical thinking which many sociologists would see as basic. His idea of social science was very much that you do history on the one hand and on the other you have an array of
concepts that sensitize such historical interpretation. *Economy
and Society* is more of an array of concepts than a series of
sociological generalizations. I don't think Weber's view of methodological individualism has really stood up to the test of time.
His methodological ideas were fairly confused, in spite of their
brilliance. And his theory of bureaucracy turns out to be quite
time-bound. The world isn't becoming more and more bureaucratic in the way Weber anticipated. He wasn't right to
focus on the 'iron cage' as the prime problem of modern civilization. And of course it is not proven that Protestantism or
Puritanism were at the origins of modern capitalism, as We-

ber claimed. It is still as disputable as it was in Weber's time. I tend to the view that the older Italian cities had most of the characteristics of what was later to become generalizable as capitalism, including a certain attitude towards the world. So no, I don't think you could say Weber has stood the test of time and that the work of the others hasn't.

Weber was a riven – and driven – personality. All through his life he struggled to reconcile contemplation and action, passion and reason, intellectual life and politics. And you find these schisms emerging in his intellectual writing as well. The tension between passion and reason is perhaps the prime theme of Weber's life, reflected in a series of personal troubles and depressions. He was a more complex person than Durkheim or Marx. Durkheim and Marx both had a project which they stuck to in spite of life's difficulties.

But there's a play between passion and reason in Marx's work as well, isn't there?

No, I don't think so. Marx thought that passion and reason could be reconciled, whereas Weber always saw them as dependent, yet contradictory.

But isn't it true that, at least to some extent, they conflict in Marx as well? Doesn't Marx struggle to reconcile a kind of historical determinism with the necessity for passion, agency, the revolutionary will?

Marx's work was also complicated. But he was more of a complex writer than a complex person – the tangled nature of his writings derives from other sources, including his moving from country to country. Famously, he began being influenced by Hegel and German classical philosophy and tried to build a radicalism on that basis. Then he had to leave Germany and when he was in exile in Paris he came across the writings of the early socialists and communists. After that he left France for England and started to read political economy. Marx's writings are made up of these various strands and he never managed to reconcile the various inheritances from these different sources.

You have spoken about the context in which Capitalism and Modern Social Theory *was written, trying, in some sense, to redeem an account of early sociology which neglected Marx. If we move forward to the 1980s, your focus shifted towards* A Contemporary Critique of Historical Materialism, *in some sense deconstructing historical materialism. In the 1990s, though, when many people want to ditch Marx comprehensively, you argue that actually it is a mistake to throw him out. In the light of that trajectory, what do you now make of Marx's contribution?*

At the time I wrote *Capitalism and Modern Social Theory*, people who weren't themselves Marxists neglected Marx and considered Marx's writings already obsolete. That is what Parsons thought, for example. Many think the same again now, for much more powerful reasons given the collapse of Communism. But my view of Marx has remained roughly the same. That is, Marx had a lot to say about the development of modern capitalism which remains valid, in terms of the origins and nature of capitalistic enterprise and the wider society framed round these. Always problematic in Marx was what he saw as his main achievement – an account of how the socialist society of the future would look, and how it would come into being. The collapse of that model shows the limitations of Marx's views about the society of the future. But Marx was right about the fractured nature of capitalism. It is a restless system which can't stay still, in which unhampered market forces tend to lead to a polarization of rich and poor, and which also tends towards oligopoly. We now live in a global capitalist civilization without the socialist alternative that Marx foresaw. Marxism as a project is dead but Marx's writings still have resonance and relevance for us.

Marx's writings also involved the claim, in part independent of whether there is to be a transition to socialism, that capitalism generates social organization based essentially upon class. Do you think that this thinking in terms of class is something else that has to be ditched?

The theme of class conflict as the motor of history certainly has to be discarded. The idea of class conflict as the driving force of historical change doesn't work. Yet capitalism does produce class divisions and they are still there. One might even talk today of a hardening of class divisions with the globalization of capitalism, although these don't quite match those identified by Marx. In the developed economies, the manual working class has shrunk dramatically. New processes of exclusion, however, have developed at the bottom of the class structure, while at the top there has emerged a global cosmopolitan class.

Isn't there a difficulty with looking at things in this way? Really, what we are talking about in contemporary capitalism is certainly still the generation of inequalities, perhaps heightened inequalities, because of the global character of capitalism and also differences in lifestyle and opportunities between people differently placed in terms of these inequalities. But one of the elements not only of Marx's view of class but surely of others was that these classes actually formed cleavages of potential political action. This does not necessarily involve the teleological idea that there is a motor of history that is driving the working class, the universal class, on to its destiny. There has also been a much more mundane and general account of class divisions as politically consequential. Now some people want to say, look, even that doesn't apply any more. So, they claim, there isn't a working class, there isn't a distinctive working-class political interest, there aren't politically potentially active classes generated by this kind of global capitalism.

I agree with most of that. Up to the period of intensifying globalization and the development of electronic communication systems, plus computerization of the world economy – that is, up until something like the early 1970s – Western societies were politicized class systems, in which the welfare state was essentially a balance of class power between labour and capital. Since then, because of the intensifying of globalization, the mobility of capital has left labour far behind. So the balance doesn't work any more. Once that balance changes, political alignments break away more and more from class divisions and the welfare state comes under strain. Labour movements become defensive in relation to the consequences of the global market place; their power is plainly limited by these changes.

I want to come back to talk about globalization more generally at a later stage. But I wonder if you think there is any potential for international political action on the basis of the 'dominated' forces or classes? One view of these changes is to say that the international class of capital (whatever that might be) is able to cohere and act in so far as it needs to, but that it is actually nationally based labour movements which have been effectively disempowered by these kinds of change.

No, at the moment I don't think there is any such counterbalancing global force in prospect, not if that means a class-based, disenfranchised international movement. I can't see any basis for that at all. The globalization of capital means that the basic moving forces of the economy aren't the result of the activities of a directive capitalistic class, which was always more of a national phenomenon than Marx thought. Nobody controls financial markets.

Isn't this picture overdrawn? National capitalists were always primarily on the receiving end of market forces rather than decision-makers. You might say that only for a comparatively short period, perhaps for twenty-five years in the post-war period, was there a co-ordinated or corporatist management of the economy which, in any sense, represented the capitalist class choosing to do what it wanted to do.

That's true. All I mean is that there was something closer to a Marxian class scenario then than there is now, even though the dynamics of inequality that Marx diagnosed are still around. But with intensifying globalization, there isn't anything recognizable as an 'upper' class or 'capitalist' class that is somehow in directive control of the flux of the global economy.

Let me put to you a Marxian alternative, one loosely identifiable with Rosa Luxemburg. This is that globalization is simply a further stage in the intensification of the contradictions of capitalism. It is a purer and more truly universal form of capitalism. The limits of capital are closer to being reached when the whole world (and all its citizens) have been brought within the ambit of a single, truly global, capitalist market economy. What Western Europe experienced in some earlier period may now reproduce itself elsewhere.

No, it can't happen now because the conditions of globalized capitalism are different. A 'purer form' of capitalism it is, but there is no dialectic of history due to create a global transition to some form of world socialism. And even if there were a global evolutionary process bound up with the limitations of capitalism, socialism is dead as a model of economic organization that would serve to overcome them.

Having looked at Durkheim, Weber and Marx in some detail, I want to raise a more general point. You have spoken about disciplines as 'imagined communities' which reconstruct their own past. Now, the three figures you identify, for all their differences, belong to a very particular time and place and gender. Do you regret that some people may have come to think that sociology is Marx, Durkheim and Weber and everything that followed on from them? Is it really possible to talk about the foundations of sociology pivoting on or issuing from these three men?

I don't think anyone would argue that these three were the only significant founders of sociology. I believed that when I wrote *Capitalism and Modern Social Theory* and haven't a different view now. If you are thinking of feminism and the influence of feminism, I still find it hard to identify a major author who would range alongside those three. Of course, what would now be regarded as feminist themes – and ones that run contrary to them – can be picked out in their writings. There is a past to be reconstructed here. Disciplines mutate as such reconstructions occur. These invented traditions don't necessarily conform to how the past actually was, as we all know.

I suppose that a critic might argue that 'the study of society' is a very ancient practice and that the reason you prefer to describe sociology as the study of modernity is because you trace the dis-

*cipline to the twenty years either side of the turn of this century.
The thinkers that you identify are writing in a particular historical place and time, which is the late nineteenth-century experience of both capitalism and a kind of modernity.*

It does depend partly on how sociology is defined. I make a
distinction between sociology and social theory, and issues of
social theory go a long way back. If sociology means something
coherent, it couldn't really refer to the study of society in general, that's much too vague. So I have always thought of sociology as reflection on the emergence of modernity.

*You have said that you now see the origins of sociology much as
you did twenty-five years ago. Are there classical figures in sociology who, on longer reflection, you think deserved a larger place
in this story?*

Simmel does. I did some work on Simmel when I was writing
Capitalism and Modern Social Theory, but I didn't fully appre-
ciate then that he offered another view of history and culture,
equivalent in interest to the other three. I still don't think that
has been rescued fully enough. People tend to think of Simmel
as the theorist of the local and the small-scale, whereas he had
a philosophy of culture and he wrote about many different
issues in philosophy, history and cultural theory. He was almost as encyclopedic a thinker as Weber. And it would obviously be easy to spin out the lexicon of sociology; there are
plenty of writers, such as Herbert Spencer, for whom, in writing a more comprehensive history of sociology, a prime place
would be found. But I wasn't writing a book of that kind.

*You've raised the question about feminism and perhaps the ab-
sence of feminist authors in this originating period. I think some-*

times critics have argued that you have not given enough weight to feminist thinkers, perhaps in the treatment of both social theory and the development of sociology. Do you think that's fair?

Well, that would depend who you had in mind as a feminist thinker and what feminism actually means . . .

Well, there are two sets of responses, I guess. One is that there are many reasons which feminists identify as to why women weren't as influential in the generation of academic discourse as men were – for example, that they didn't get the same access to institutions of higher education. But there is also an argument that, in some ways, this is an excuse used by men who don't want to recognize the fact that there is a 'hidden' history of women writing sociology or writing about society in these kinds of period which simply didn't get recognized for those same sorts of reason.

Well, there may be but I'd be interested to hear what it is. As I said, one can look at the writings of key thinkers from the point of view of what they neglected and what their views were about certain issues relevant to feminism. But I'm not sure one can do much more than that.

What do you think of the more general claim that feminist thought or feminist ideas or feminist sensibilities are not sufficiently reflected in the way you've talked about the character of capitalism or modernity or whatever?

Well, that to some extent may be true. But I don't think you could trace out a history of neglected figures whose ideas now need to be taken into account as somehow crucial to the formation of sociology.

Could we go back to a question I raised earlier? Sociology is often described as the study of society but you choose to make it apply to the study of modernity. Why?

Well, because otherwise sociology would be just another synonym for the social sciences. There has to be a division of labour in the social sciences. Understanding sociology as the reflexive analysis of modernity is a useful way to distinguish it from anthropology, for example.

You might want to say that 'the whole of the social sciences' is too broad, but in some sense what you do with your definition is simply to delimit historically what you will look at, but you don't lessen the breadth of a sociological approach. Some people would say that the definitive social science for studying modernity is economics, because we are really talking about society since the rise of capitalism and the centrality of market processes.

But no one could define modernity simply in economic terms.

No, but then sociology isn't much narrowed, is it?

Well, it's much narrower than sociology as the study of society. Then it does appear to include almost everything. Sociology defines down the object of its study in temporal terms, or as the study of a particular type of society and its impact in the world rather than 'society' in a very generalized way. That's why I make a distinction between sociology and social theory. I think it is quite sensible to say that some of the tasks of social theory are very generalized, as when you are reflecting, for example, on how to use the concept of society or culture, or whatever it might be. But sociology I see as a narrower field than that.

Can I ask an associated question, which is to do with sociology and economics? One of the ways people have tried to delimit sociology is to say that sociologists study society and economists study the economy. This is not very satisfactory but I guess one aspect of globalization, some people would say, is that economics or economic characteristics seem to be increasingly important in people's day-to-day lives, or at least they seem to be more apparent to people in their day-to-day lives. At the same time, there has been a tendency over the last twenty-five years in the social sciences for economics to make something of a take-over bid for explanation, that is, through the general application of rational choice, or using the model of the rational egoistic actor. I wondered if you think there is a relationship between the increasing prominence of economics in day-to-day life and this bid for economics, as a discipline, to take over social explanation. And, in general terms, what do you make of rational choice explanations?

There is a relationship, but it is not one which just reflects recent changes, because economists were already trying to do that in the nineteenth century. And there has been, as it were, a continuing dialogue between economics and the rest of the social sciences about issues of explanation, individualism and rationality. Durkheim and Marx were both trying to criticize classical economics from the point of view of its limitations as an overall account of social development. I wouldn't see things very differently now. Economics is important not only because of its ideas and theories, but because to some degree it is actually bound up with producing economic reality. If you are a business person you have to think in terms of the categories of economics, cost analysis and so forth. But economic thought can't offer a framework for the understanding of modern institutions as a whole.

I don't know how true it is in sociology but certainly in political science, I think there has been a very clear change in the last twenty years or so, away from traditional, constitutional explanations, or indeed political sociology explanations of, for example, voting behaviour or parties' activities, and an attempt to bring these under the rubric of rational choice. Certainly, rational choice has been applied to sociological things like choosing marriage partners and lying and cheating. There has been a colonization which is something at least quantitatively different, if not qualitatively different, from the impact that economic ideas had previously outside the discipline. In its most extreme form, it fosters the attempt to explain all forms of social action in terms of the calculative behaviour of rational egoists.

We should separate out rational choice from economic theory because the two are not the same; and neo-classical theory, in spite of its preeminence, is only one type of economic theory. So there is quite a distance between say Gary Becker, who does claim that a whole variety of activities can be analysed in terms of neo-classical economic theory, and someone like Jon Elster, who is working with broader models of rationality, using economic notions but not deploying the whole armoury of neo-classical economic theory. Yet in neither version do these ideas have more than limited purchase. Elster seems now to recognize limits similar to those identified in the debates of a hundred years ago, by Durkheim among others. In *The Cement of Society*, for example, he accepts that a theory of cultural values and cultural frameworks can't be generated from acts of individual exchange. While these perspectives are certainly influential in political science, more so than in sociology or anthropology, they aren't dominant, but represent one particular viewpoint.

It probably is more true of political science than it is of sociology, but it is very widely applied, for example, in accounts of how bureaucracies work, which is a theme in classical, organizational sociology. This is the kind of discourse which lies behind new public management and those kinds of reform.

I have some sympathy with rational choice theory, because it recognizes that people are mostly knowledgeable about what they do, and make choices, even if those choices often rebound on them. So I don't find the impact of rational choice thinking surprising or in any way worrying. But generalizing neo-classical economic theory as *the* theory of social science won't work. There is probably going to be quite a strong reaction against the dominance of such thinking in economics itself anyway, as Paul Ormerod and others argue.

A final question about the state of contemporary sociology. Sociology has always had its vigorous critics. Someone who was basically sympathetic but critical might, I guess, say that sociology has rather lost its way. Much of its time seems to be taken up with arcane methodological disputes about what can be said about the social world, and, on the other hand, those areas where it is applied empirically are maybe increasingly on the margins or about the margins and the marginalized. These may be very important issues, but if one thinks about the classic strengths of British sociology, they have lain in accounts of the sociology of work, of economic life and of social inequality. Is it fair to say that sociology has this tendency to go off to either the margins or the epistemological, and that a great chunk of social explanation just doesn't get done in the way it should?

I don't think so. First of all, there are bound to be debates about the nature of social reality. That's a part of what doing sociology is. In that respect, I prefer the situation of sociology to that of economics, where there isn't so much methodological probing. People say sociology has lost its way and there is a crisis in sociology and so forth, but that is partly precisely because sociology has become so central to our lives. People no longer see sociology for what it is, because most of the debates that occupy people *are* sociological debates now. They are about crime, cities, families, sexuality, individualism, social solidarity, the limits of industrialism, the changing nature of work. These are all core sociological topics. When the media discuss these issues, they depend on social research. Because such topics are so widely discussed, to some degree they lose the sense of being a separate intellectual endeavour which is sociology. There is a more collaborative kind of reflection on social life now than there used to be, something which is itself a sociological topic of some interest.

There are a couple of possible responses, aren't there? One is to say that while it is certainly important to be reflective about what the enterprise is and how one perceives the social world, that process has simply become too large a part of what sociologists do. The other is that, though the labels aren't terribly important, in some sense you are making a parallel claim to the economist's: that it is all sociology now. But actually a lot of the work on disclosing forms of social and economic inequality and those kinds of thing is now done by economists, perhaps more than by sociologists.

I wouldn't agree. As I said earlier, professional social scientists now live in a world of multiple knowledge-producers. Economics isn't in a particularly different situation from sociology in that respect. It has more of a technical apparatus maybe, which is less easy to penetrate for the outsider.

So, you think that sociologists, or people doing sociology, under whatever label, are still engaged in those concerns about the changing character of the family, questions about sexuality, questions about changing the nature of working patterns and working lives and all those kinds of thing?

Yes. I still see sociology as defined through these issues and sociological work as absolutely vital to a civilized view of the world in relation to them. We're living through a big, big period of change and no one knows quite what to make of it. Sociologists should play a key role in analysing all this.

Interview Three

Structuration Theory

CHRISTOPHER PIERSON   *The relationship between agency and structure and, paralleling that, between voluntarism and determinism is amongst the most ubiquitous and difficult issues in all social theory. In a number of texts in the late 1970s and early 1980s, culminating in the publication of* The Constitution of Society *in 1984, you developed your own distinctive resolution of this issue under the rubric of the theory of structuration. Perhaps I could begin by asking how you understand the traditional problem of structure and agency in social theory.*

ANTHONY GIDDENS   It isn't a 'traditional problem', at least expressed in these terms. In the past it was usually seen as a dualism between individual and society, or the actor and the social system. Thinking about this traditional question of the relationship between the individual and society lay at the origin of the idea of structuration. I felt these were all unelaborated notions. People would speak of the individual as though it was obvious what 'the individual' was and quite often the same was true of 'society'. I wanted to break them down and give them more substance. The term 'structuration' I originally borrowed from French – I don't think it was used in English before I appropriated it. I wanted to place an emphasis on the active flow of social life. We should see social life not just as 'society' out there or just the product of 'the individual' here, but as a series of ongoing activities and practices that people carry on, which at the same time reproduce larger institutions. That was the original thought and from there I tried to elaborate each of the key terms, precisely by speaking of 'agency' and 'structure'. I put the idea of recurrent social practices at the core of what social sciences are about, rather than either starting with 'the individual' or starting with 'society'.

The Constitution of Society is not necessarily the easiest book. Could you give some indication, in fairly straightforward terms, of how the theory of structuration resolves the dualism between structure and agency?

This depends on two things really. The first is rethinking the notion of structure. I wanted to get away from the characteristic Anglo-Saxon way of conceptualizing structure, where structure is some given form, even a visible form of some sort. But I also sought to get away from the idea that agency is just contained within the individual. I wanted to see it as more of a flow of people's actions and to connect it with attributes of self-consciousness. Within certain limits, speaking a language shows us something about what the relationship between them might be. In other words, language has structure, language has form, but it isn't visible and it is only 'there' in so far as it actually forms part of what people do in their day-to-day use of it. That is what I call the recursive quality of language. I didn't claim that society 'is like a language', as the structuralists used to say; but language gives us key clues as to how recursiveness happens. 'Society' can be understood as a complex of recurrent practices which form institutions. Those practices depend upon the habits and forms of life which individuals adopt. Individuals don't just 'use' these in their activity but these life practices constitute what that activity is.

You talk in some places about structural effects and these being a better way of describing the impact of structure. Are 'structural effects' simply a euphemism for some kind of structure which is observable or has some existence other than through these perceived effects?

The structural properties of societies and social systems are real properties, but at the same time they have no physical existence. They are real properties in the sense in which they depend upon the routine qualities of people's actions and they can be very fixed or 'hard'. I don't want to discard the Durkheimian point that society is a structured phenomenon and that the structural properties of a group or a society have effects upon the way people act, feel and think. But when we look at what those structures are, they are obviously not like the physical qualities of the external world. They depend upon regularities of social reproduction. Language has this incredibly fixed form. You can't go against even the most apparently minute rules of the English language without getting very strong reactions from other speakers. But at the same time, language doesn't exist anywhere, or it only exists in its instantiations in writing or speaking. Much the same thing is true for social life in general. That is, society only has form and that form only has effects on people in so far as structure is produced and reproduced in what people do. This to me applies right through from the most trivial glance you might give someone to the most globalized of systems.

You seem to be drawing an analogy between social practices and language, where all one can see is particular performances but these give expression to an underlying or underpinning structure.

I wouldn't quite regard it as an analogy because language is obviously such a key part of what people actually do. It exemplifies a large part of what social life is like because it is a core part of what social life is.

But you don't want to say that all social structures are expressed in or take a linguistic form?

No, I don't say that qualities of language express all other aspects of social life. Structure is primarily expressed in the things that people do in a regularized and institutionalized way. Much of what we do in everyday life is governed by what I call practical consciousness – 'going on' with the rules and conventions of social life.

In the way you perceive it, must structures always be an expression of action? Is there always an agent involved in the reconstitution or reproduction of structures?

Well, it seems to me there is, yes. If one sees agency as essentially the capability to have done otherwise, the whole of social life rests upon it. Even someone who is threatened by a bullet from a gun remains an agent in a philosophical sense. Many social scientists have failed to acknowledge what is obvious to any lay person – that we are conscious, intentional beings, who, among other things, read sociology and reflect upon its findings.

What would you say to an unreconstructed structuralist who insisted that the agency of which you speak doesn't really exist and that where an agent appears to be making a choice, in fact there is something else behind her or him, which is driving her or him to choose in a particular kind of way? Such a structuralist might say that you have the appearance of action because you have the appearance of choices, but in some sense there is always something behind pulling the strings, a ventriloquist putting words in the mouth of a puppet.

Well, your structuralist would have to tell me what this 'something' is. Assuming they aren't unconscious emotions, which structuralists aren't talking about in this context, what could these forces possibly be?

Let's look at an example. If you asked an eighteen-year-old, male, working-class Catholic Glaswegian whether he supported Celtic or Rangers, you might say that he had the option to choose either, but you would have some grounds for confidence in your prediction that he wouldn't follow the Blues.

One mustn't confuse the logical notion of agency with the sociological notion of socialization. One is part of an explanation of what it is to be a human being in the first place, while the other is much more an account of what actually happens to certain kinds of person in certain kinds of setting as a result of social influences around them. 'Social influences' aren't like causal connections in nature. There are certain Catholic Glaswegians who don't support Celtic and probably some who don't even follow football at all.

So, presumably, as well, you wouldn't give any particular status to an agent's own account of his or her reasons for making a particular choice? So if, in this example, the young man said he supported Celtic because they were the greatest team in the world, you wouldn't necessarily take his account at face value.

Well, I don't know about that because I give more weight to what people say about what they do than most sociologists. On the whole, people tend to know more about why they act as they do than many sociologists have supposed. When someone says something about why he or she supports a particular football team, you could ask further questions which might elicit responses such as 'my dad's always supported Celtic' or 'I come from this particular area of the town' or 'there has always been this connection between Catholics and Celtic'. I don't want at all to deny that there are social influences that affect people's behaviour, but they do so only via the attitudes and views that they hold.

Let me pursue a slightly different question about structures. Is unemployment and the impact of unemployment a structural effect? I'm thinking about the ways in which structural features of the world present themselves to individuals. For an unemployed person, the phenomenon of unemployment, which is an expression that has been drawn into everyday life, may appear as a powerful external force or an external reality, the limits of which she or he feels.

I wouldn't dispute that at all – it certainly is true for an individual facing the labour market. But I don't think that in any way compromises the logic of the relation between agency and structure. Agency doesn't mean that the world is plastic to the will of the individual. Moreover, there is a strong reflective, developmental and linguistic aspect to what unemployment is. Unemployment doesn't just exist. You have to have a certain form of life for it to have any meaning – essentially that of a modern market-based society.

Couldn't you be an unemployed person because of the way in which other actors, state actors or statisticians for example, define your status without necessarily knowing yourself to be so?

No, you have to be aware of it under some description or another. Of course, any activity can be redefined. Someone who is retired isn't 'unemployed', even though 'from the outside' there is no difference. There is a difference only because that is the way the economic order is currently organized through the concepts that constitute what that system is.

Let me take a slightly different economic example. I am really pushing a point which some critics have made, which is that perhaps the idea of structure isn't sufficiently embracing of things in the social world which might constitute structural effects. So if we considered something like population density, something which has an impact upon the economy and thence upon social structure, would that constitute an aspect of structure in your sense? It's not really an aspect of agency, is it?

I just don't see what the problem is. Structure only exists in so far as people do things knowledgeably and do them in certain contexts that have particular consequences. Those consequences are often ones that they don't themselves foresee or even know about – but it is their regular happening, their reproduction – which makes them structural and allows us to talk of structural effects. Structural effects are causal, but only in so far as they are mediated through the kinds of property that I am describing. There isn't any other way in which population density, for example, has structural effects, except in so far as it is organized through what people actually do. What other causal properties are there?

So if I take a final example of this kind, which I guess you're not going to find problematic either, is the level of technological knowledge within a given society an aspect of structure?

Well, it certainly exemplifies structural properties of societies. Technology does nothing except as implicated in the actions of human beings.

But it does delimit a range of choices for social actors. Social actors are in some sense constrained in agency by these aspects of a social or physical environment.

That's true of anything physical. It's true whether you have a computer on your desk or not.

Somebody might suggest that your conception of structure and the way in which that acts as a framework of either constraint or empowerment for individuals is too limited if it doesn't take into account these kinds of aspect of the physical environment and so on.

But it does. The mistake of some of my critics is to imply that I think that structure is somehow in people's heads because I say it is produced recursively by what people do. Social systems only exist because people do what they do from day to day. They do what they do in lots of different contexts, including physical contexts, which are strongly relevant to the possibilities and constraints facing any individual or group. Yet social structure plainly just doesn't have the same kind of existence as physical structure, nor do its causal effects, they can't do. We live in a physical world which has causal effects in the sense that you can't just walk straight through a wall. The causal effects of structural properties of human institutions, by contrast, are there simply because they are produced and reproduced in everyday actions. Ultimately, they depend upon convention, which is both the means and the outcome of such actions.

Convention – what people do, what they do in their day-to-day lives – can have very severe constraining effects, of course, on what is possible for any individual. Language is the same; yet language is the means of doing all sorts of things one couldn't accomplish without it. Although it has a physical presence, technology is no different: it is constraining and enabling. It depends upon relationships between reasoning agents, who have various habits and conventions and do things. The fact that as they do these things in relation to machines and so forth these are the stuff out of which structural properties are constructed. At the same time, structural properties make those actions possible. People can only act conventionally because of mutual understanding of convention. You can't just invent your own conventions. Use of convention, in language or more broadly, normally depends upon 'practical consciousness' – what Wittgenstein called our capacity to 'go on' in the diversity of contexts of social life. A great deal of social research just writes out the area of practical consciousness. People are treated as less knowledgeable than they really are, because the limits of what they know are assumed to be what they can say about what they do. But what actors can say about what they do, and why they do it, is only one small part of the immense knowledgeability involved in the conduct of everyday life. If we go back to computers, computers have this enormous informational power, yet even the most powerful computers can't do what human agents routinely do at each and every moment of the day. They can't pick up the most casual aspects of conversational talk, for example. They may in the future possibly be able to do it but at the moment they can't. You have to know an enormous amount to be an agent, and this is central to being an agent. Without such knowledgability there wouldn't be structures, there wouldn't be institutions, because that knowledge is the key to social reproduction, the only reason structural properties exist at all.

But you don't want entirely to privilege actors' own account of what they are doing or how they are behaving?

No. The choice isn't between what people say about why they act as they do, on the one hand, and some kind of causal force that makes them act as they do, on the other. In between these there is the knowledgeable use of convention in practical consciousness – and there is power. I have always tried to see power as an elemental part of the logic of the social sciences too. So it's agency, structure and power really. Agency is an elemental basis of power. It is the capability to do otherwise and that is the basis of power, no matter how large-scale any given structure of power may be.

But to some extent that compromises the capacity of some agents to act out their agency. You talked about agents even with an extremely limited range of options still being agents because they still have a choice to make. But, of course, the range of those options may not be very large or at all attractive.

That's why in some situations (a person pointing a gun at your head, for example), we say someone 'has no choice'. But such a description always presumes motivation. If you didn't value your life at all, it would be of no significance that someone is pointing a gun at you. It isn't the same as the use of physical force, even if we can properly say 'X was forced to act this way at the point of a gun.' All social constraints are only constraints in terms of motives or interests actors have. The same applies to collectivities as well. Say a firm makes a business decision. Normally, business people accept the logic of the wider economy – and that is part of what the wider economy is, it is a constitutive phenomenon. There would be no economy unless people acted in this way.

Of course, it can all collapse – as is true of elemental social order. I am impressed with the thoughts of some linguists about the closeness of everyday life to chaos. Disorder and anger set in very quickly if people don't follow even the simplest conversational routines. You do have to show yourself to be an agent the whole time for people to accept you as an agent. Agency presumes constraints – but what is harder to understand is that constraint also presumes agency.

On the other hand, there are some very large-scale, agent-driven, non-centrally controlled structures like markets which in some sense are perceived to be chaotic but in other senses seem to be highly structured and also, I guess, vulnerable themselves to going violently off the rails.

There is a very interesting issue here. All social life is agent-controlled in the sense that to be a human being is to monitor one's behaviour constantly in relation to that of others – there is no time out from this process, which is simply chronic. On the other hand, vast areas of social life aren't agent-controlled, if that means consciously directed by anyone. Markets have shown us the limits of directive control in this second sense. Markets aren't simply the 'outcome' of millions of individuals taking individual decisions to buy, sell, save and so forth. They have highly structured properties which – as structuration theory underlines – are simultaneously the consequence and the means of actions individuals carry out. Moreover, markets in the contemporary sense presume a certain style of discourse, which agents incorporate in what they do, even if when asked they might not be able to say very much about what a market is.

But the kind of knowledge that an actor at some point within the market has to have of the way in which market economies operate is really very small. Children go to a sweet shop and know that if they don't hand over their money they are not going to get the Mars bar. But they don't know about the way in which, behind that, an international economy operates and processes of production and exchange take place.

Even a child actually knows a lot more about what money is than he or she would be able to say about the nature of money. The child probably knows quite a lot even about commodity exchanges, since she or he might easily have been inclined simply to steal the sweets. In any simple transaction like that, there is actually an enormous number of complex things going on. They aren't revealed in what is actually said in the transaction. People have historically had to learn lots of things for a market society to exist and continue, and also have had to change their values and so on. A child buys something in a sweet shop, it's obviously only one small element in a larger totality. The child could be buying something in a sweet shop within only a local exchange, without a global market. It's a big thing when the sweet comes from China rather than from a hundred yards down the road.

A question about the externality of structures. One of the things you resist is giving too architectural an account or image of structures. One of the classical things about structures is that they should have a reality which if not touchable is at least perceivable. Now, I'm not quite sure what Durkheim's principle of treating social facts as things would or wouldn't mean in this context, but we know that for individual actors, these kinds of social structure and social constraint can be extremely powerful. They might almost be as powerful as physical constraints. Social forces may be as powerful as actual physical coercion. So, are these structures, in some sense, external things for individual actors?

Yes, of course, they are for a situated individual. The individual doesn't include within himself or herself the whole gamut of social life. I can't see anything problematic about that at all.

Well, I was interested in the character of structures or structural properties because they are not tangible physical things in a way that objects in the external world are, but they may act upon the individual with the same force as those objects in the external world. What is the nature of the distinction between them?

The distinction between them is pretty fundamental. There are only structural forces, to repeat, in so far as there are established conventions that people follow. There are structures only in so far as people constantly reproduce those conventions in what they do and they give structured form to institutions. Institutions incorporate at the same time forms of power but they are simply not like physical structures.

Are agents, in this kind of conception of the relationship between agency and structure, always individual human agents?

One can sometimes speak of collectivities as if they were agents, but this is only metaphorical. It presumes certain qualities which they have in the aggregate – firms oriented towards profit, for example, or hospitals concerned with curing people. But the only true agents in history are human individuals.

So a social class might be a collectivity of people who have the same relationship to, say, ownership of means of production and maybe act in particular collective ways because of a commonality, but you wouldn't be happy with the idea that they have agency?

Some social thinkers have spoken in this way, but I don't think many would regard social classes as actors. They are much more likely to see business firms or organizations in that way, because these have certain institutionalized values and aspirations. For example, the law treats them as agents, and in so far as the law does so, to some extent this becomes constitutive of what they are. If the law defines a business firm as an agent, it gives it certain opportunities and also places certain constraints on it.

I suppose there was once a dimension in sociology – and I'm thinking here not so much of class as of the sociology of crowd behaviour and those kinds of thing – which wanted to suggest there were forms of action which belonged to the group, could only be perceived or understood or explained in that context . . .

But they were nearly always actually linked to the unconscious; that was Freud's group psychology, Le Bon's treatment of the crowd and so on. They saw these groups as the collective unconscious in action, but not as agents in the sense I am referring to.

How about comprehending social change within structuration and structuration theory? In other places, you obviously take issue with historical materialism as an explanatory scheme and with evolutionism much more generally. Is there a space in your account for large-scale, perhaps society-wide, systemic forms of social change?

I wouldn't just pick out social change, because we have to explain stability *and* change, or constancy *and* change. Change doesn't exist as something on its own. In structuration theory, I argue that the possibility of change is there in every moment of social life, but a key part of social life is social reproduction. So change and constancy are somehow directly bound up with one another. If we ask wider questions about, say, why feudalism collapsed, one can't answer those on a logical level – we must look for more directly sociological, economic and political interpretations of what happened. I don't claim to derive those from structuration theory as such. What I have always been against is any kind of 'single-factor' theory of change, such as that economic factors 'in the last instance' determine major episodes of historical transformation.

You might feel that this is a question which you have answered already, but let me put it to you directly. There is a view that structuration theory generates more sophisticated principles and a nuanced duality of structure and agency, but that it doesn't overcome the most primitive and deep-seated problem of structure and agency, which is about whether there are causes outside of individual agents which determine or influence or condition the way in which they act.

I think it does. There are really only two sources of structural effects. One, as I say, consists in the regularity of conventions that people follow; the other concerns the unintended consequences of what they do, which, however, rebound on their future actions.

We can't make any sense of social life without something like the view that I am taking. I don't see what the alternative is. I can see failed alternatives, as it were, like Durkheim and social facts, or even the methodology of neo-classical economics. People might not like the concepts I use, and may prefer say a version by Bourdieu or somebody else, but that is just what social life is like. It is continually contingently reproduced by knowledgeable human agents – that's what gives it fixity and that's what also produces change.

There is one other thing which is slightly tangential to structuration which we could maybe address at this point: that is the treatment of time and space and time-space distanciation. Why do you think these issues are neglected in classical sociology, in so far as you think they are, and why is it important to introduce them here?

There are two aspects to this. It is important to see that all agency unfolds in time and therefore is a flow, not just an aggregate of individual actions. Therefore temporality is bound up with human agency and so also is spatiality; because you can't be a human agent without having a body and a body occupies a physical space and it orients itself towards others in a physical context. In that sense time and space are theorized as part of structuration theory. But a second aspect is studying time and space as a way of understanding more concretely the properties of social systems. It illuminates what different kinds of social system are like – how they manage to organize themselves across time and space, and also how people conceptualize time and space.

Lévi-Strauss was right to say that most social thinkers tend to equate time and change and that is an empirical as well as a conceptual mistake. For most of human history, the most striking thing is constancy rather than change. Only at a certain period, relatively recent in historical time, is there an injection of dynamism into history, that does seem to depend upon new relationships between time, space and power which Lévi-Strauss teased out. It is from thinking about his ideas that I got the notion of 'time-space distanciation' – the capability of social systems to 'stretch' across time and space, rather than being localized. I was also influenced by the writings of geographers and I made some effort to incorporate ideas drawn from human geography into social theory.

Is there a reason why the classical sociological tradition was weak in its treatment of time and space?

The equation of time with change is one thing, so that time was assumed to be inseparable from change – 'history' is thought of as going from somewhere to somewhere. As opposed to the issue of time, spatial metaphors and some sense of the composition of space are quite important in classical social theory. Durkheim, for example, knew the work of social geographers and wrote reviews of their writings in the *Année sociologique*. Much of his work has spatial connotations, as for example in his discussion of ritual ceremonial space.

Do you think functionalism really operated with a conception of timeless change or changeless time?

The methodology of functionalism certainly depends upon abstracting from time. Giving a functionalist account of a social item means showing how that item relates to other aspects of a system so as to form a functioning whole. Functionalism as a consequence has little sensitivity to problems of time. One could say the same of agency. Consider for instance the classic discussion of functionalism by R.K. Merton. Merton uses the rain dance of the Hopi Indians of New Mexico as an example in giving an account of functional explanation. The Hopi believe the dance brings rain. We know that it doesn't, so we look for some other explanation of why they act as they do – and this is the functionalist one. The rain dance has the function of ensuring social cohesion. But this treats the Hopi as ignorant of what they are up to. Participants in most ceremonials, after all, have some sense of the various ends they might serve. Moreover, showing that the rain dance fosters social solidarity cannot possibly be an explanation of the actions of the Hopi unless at least some of them sense that this is so and act accordingly.

Are there other issues which structuration theory raises which we have not talked about? Perhaps, practical consciousness?

Practical consciousness is a key notion for me because it connects people's everyday knowledgeability with the structural nature of social systems, as discussed earlier. Most social life depends upon 'going on' in the context of convention.

Does that account of knowledgeable actors, 'going on in the world' and practical consciousness, leave space for a notion of ideology?

Yes, it does. The idea of ideology is obviously a contested one. For me ideology concerns how ideas are drawn in to support differential power – and such ideas may be taken-for-granted concepts which form part of practical consciousness. Ideology has no content apart from its relationship to power.

Ideology should be thought of in the context of the whole approach to social science method we have been talking about. It doesn't only include the grand systems of ideas, such as nationalism or religious doctrines. Some of the most entrenched forms of ideology are grounded in everyday convention – in practical consciousness and in day-to-day talk.

Interview Four

Modernity

CHRISTOPHER PIERSON   *I would like to spend some time exploring your ideas on modernity. In your textbook* Sociology *you describe this discipline as 'the study of modernity' and since 1990 you have published a number of books which are concerned with different aspects of modernity. Perhaps you might begin by explaining what you understand modernity to be and why it is qualitatively different from previous forms of society.*

ANTHONY GIDDENS   At its simplest, modernity is a shorthand term for modern society or industrial civilization. Portrayed in more detail, it is associated with (1) a certain set of attitudes towards the world, the idea of the world as open to transformation by human intervention; (2) a complex of economic institutions, especially industrial production and a market economy; (3) a certain range of political institutions, including the nation-state and mass democracy. Largely as a result of these characteristics, modernity is vastly more dynamic than any previous type of social order. It is a society – more technically, a complex of institutions – which unlike any preceding culture lives in the future rather than in the past.

The classical sociological writers we have already discussed were all concerned in different ways with the historical changes you identify with modernity. In various ways and to varying degrees, you have suggested that they all got parts of this story wrong. Would it be fair to suggest that, of the classical writers you discussed in Capitalism and Modern Social Theory, *it was Weber who came closest to seeing what modernity was about, with the idea of the disillusionment or disenchantment of the world and the end of traditional forms of authority and ways of understanding?*

It would be quite right to see these as key aspects of the modern world. But I wouldn't say Weber is any more important than the other classical authors. Unfashionable though it might be, I would still look to Marx because of the centrality of capitalism to the wider framework of modernity. Modern society is one in which economic influences have a more distinguishable and profound effect than they do in previous forms of society and these are structured around capitalistic institutions. Obviously, Weber spoke of capitalism too, but in rather different terms.

Certainly, it is hard to read Marx without having a very strong sense of dynamism.

Well, Marx was right to say that other economic systems haven't had this constant expansionary quality. This is not just expansion across space, obviously, but expansion in terms of constant technological innovation and the drive to improve productivity.

You have suggested that Marx has perhaps the most to say about this process. You seem to argue that Marx was right to see capi-

*talism as dynamic, but wrong in thinking that this dynamic was
carrying capitalism towards its own exhaustion.*

As I argued earlier, Marx was a perceptive analyst of the capitalist economy. He underestimated his own contribution to
describing capitalism, its cyclical character, the idea of the
commodity form and the nature of exchange relationships.
He was wrong to suppose capitalism would mutate into socialism.

You write in The Consequences of Modernity *of four basic institutional dimensions of modernity, which along with capitalism
would include surveillance, industrialism and military power.
Would you perhaps say something briefly about those other aspects?*

The emergence of modernity is first of all the creation of a
modern economic order, that is, a capitalistic economic order.
But modern society also involves the formation of a distinctive
kind of state and, more generally, distinctive kinds of organization. These depend essentially upon the structuring of information. That is why I use the idea of 'surveillance' – borrowed
from Foucault – as the way in which information systems are
constructed to form new systems of administrative power. The
modern state is the prime example of this process.

I think of military power as being, analytically at least, sepa-
rable from these other dimensions of modernity. There are
major changes in the nature of war and the military from about
the late eighteenth century onwards, with the development of
mass warfare – this is a different form of military power from
previous types of system. I separate industry from capitalism,
and from the other dimensions of modernity, since it refers
to the technological base of modern society. It is about the

development of a machine-based civilization, geared to the progress of science and technology.

I use these four dimensions quite a lot. I don't mean to say they are all wholly independent of or equivalent to one another. I tend to think that the expansion of capitalism is the most significant driving force of change. But nation-states also operate independently, and form a partially independent locus of power. They have their own military adventures and there is an enormous amount of change in science and technology which isn't just market-driven.

You talk about modernity being 'discontinuous'. Is there really a discontinuity in the forms and logics of military power from premodern to modern societies?

I think there is. Not just mass war, as I mentioned – normally involving civilian populations as well as combatants – but the nature of the military shifted. Military technology also altered under the influence of the other characteristics of modernity. It became much more of a machine-type thing – the machine gun itself was the exemplar. Uniforms used to be a form of display – revealing oneself to the enemy. Later uniforms became a way of hiding, as camouflage. There are large-scale changes within army discipline and armies start to look more like machines themselves.

I have a question about periodization within modernity. You could say that some of these changes actually take place within *the period that you are thinking of as modernity; for example, the change in uniforms, battlefield tactics and the mechanization of war.*

One can't periodize such things very accurately – as with the other dimensions of modernity. Modern institutions became consolidated somewhere around about the late eighteenth century, but plainly a much more extended process of change was involved as well, stretching backwards and forwards. I don't think that's incompatible with seeing modernity as discontinuous with previous forms of society, but these transitions didn't occur overnight.

You also raise, in the context of discussing modernity, the idea of time and space and the organization of time and space. You raise the idea of disembedded and re-embedded social arrangements and social relationships. Could you say something more about that?

A feature of modernity is that distant events and actions have a constant effect on our lives, and a constantly increasing one too. That is what I mean by disembedding, the 'lifting out' of forms of life, their recombination across time and space,but also the reconstitution of the contexts from which they came. An artisan working in a local context and producing for a local market is embedded in the local area and local community. With the development of more of an international division of labour, this changes – economic exchange becomes more and more lifted out of the local community and recombined across time and space. The 'local' reflects much larger processes, which in some part reshape it, perhaps in a dramatic way. What happens in the economy happens in many other areas of life as well: processes of 'disembedding' and 're-embedding' or 'lifting out' and 'pushing back'. Today, in a period of intensifying globalization, these effects are more pronounced than before.

Again, is this a process which has always been there under modernity and is simply intensifying, or is it something 'new' under late modernity? Mightn't one argue that the international migra-

tion of industries, and the consequent deindustrialization and deskilling of local industries, can be seen as well in the nineteenth century as in the latter part of the twentieth?

Disembedding and re-embedding convey the idea of the restructuring and reforming of relationships across space and time – and therefore how different forms of social system are constituted. There are an indefinite number of examples we could draw from trade or whatever. But there are two main historical transitions in which there is a 'leap forward'. One is the emergence of the first civilizations – Greece, Rome, traditional China – they organized time and space differently from oral cultures, cultures without writing. The more or less universal association of civilization with writing isn't fortuitous. With the advent of writing, information can be stored over time, and goods too; new systems of power are generated through these. In the case of modernity, these traits are more inclusive and far-reaching than in any previous civilization. Many authors speak of the emergence of an information society today, but in a broad sense there has been an 'information society' for several centuries, because of printing and the mass production of printed materials, and the relatively early development of electronic communication. These alter not just the way people communicate with one another, but how whole societies are organized. The invention in the mid-nineteenth century of the first form of electronic communication, the Morse code, injected something completely new again. Before Morse, someone always had to go somewhere to carry information from one point to another – this was the beginning of the electronic age.

Does the rise of electronic communication, which is at least intensified in the present period, prescribe a particular kind of societal development?

No. I think it is just one aspect of disembedding really. But it was certainly driven in some part by the perceived demands of the new society. There was an active search for quicker and more effective forms of communication across time and space.

Sometimes, this process is given a rather technologically determinist spin . . .

I don't think so. I do see communication, and changes in systems of communication, as particularly important to the constitution and development of societies. Electronic communication is more important, and from an earlier time, than many people assume.

You wouldn't have to go very far, though, to find people who would say that the introduction of information technology is what creates a global market economy which, in turn, has very particular social consequences.

We're back here to technological determinism. Information technology is bound up with the workings of a global economy, but many other forces are involved, including the driving power of capitalism and industrialism.

Your account also places considerable emphasis upon the linked ideas of trust and risk as distinctive characteristics, or at least taking a distinctive format, within modernity.

They take on distinctive forms. Trust and risk again concern the topic of time and space – they are both ways of organizing future time. The notion of risk comes from the early modern period. It is a marker of the attempt to break away from the past and confront an open future. The idea of risk seems first to have emerged in two contexts: from the explorers as they set off to previously unknown areas, and from the activities of the early mercantile capitalists. In each case there were new and uncharted territories to explore – the unknown lands and the uncharted territory of the future.

Risk has to be separated from hazard or danger. Risk is about the active assessment of future hazards, and becomes a more pervasive notion the more a society seeks to live in the future and shape it actively. The concept of risk becomes generalized with the rise of modernity, as does the idea of insurance. Insurance and safety are the other side of risk.

Trust is also about the binding of time and space, because trust means giving commitment to a person, group or system across future time. The notion of trust also tends to be a modern notion. Obviously there are forms of what we would now call trust in traditional cultures. Most such cultures, however, don't have a notion of trust – or risk.

Risk and trust are closely bound up with one another. Trust – in a person, or in a system, such as a banking system – can be a means of coping with risk, while acceptance of risk can be a means of generating trust.

How about risk and another term, opportunity? Do you think that maybe opportunity is a stronger aspect in early modernity and that risk is in some sense a later-maturing kind of sensibility?

I do. But first let me mention something else. There are two aspects of risk, and there are two literatures of risk which aren't very often brought together. First, there is risk as a positive element of investment decisions and risk-taking, as a dynamic aspect of what markets are about. Much of the literature on risk in economics quite rightly treats risk as a positive phenomenon. Risk is always negative in one sense, because it refers to outcomes one wants to avoid; but the active acceptance of risk, and risk management, are at the core of the modern market economy. Risk isn't by any means only something to be minimized – and, of course, we all know the positive elements of risks from mountaineering and other risk-taking activities in which people willingly engage. The second literature of risk sees risk only in relation to security and safety – it is prominent in the areas of environmental-ism, health and so forth. These two perspectives of risk have to be brought together. For in the global era the influence of risk has become generalized. We live in a 'risk culture', which is to be explained by the radicalizing and generalizing of mo-dernity. Various changes are leading or forcing us to think more and more in terms of risk. One is the dwindling hold of tradition. The more social activities are structured by what has been done in the past, the more people tend to think in terms of fate. The more we take active decisions about future events, the more, whether people are aware of it or not, they think in terms of risk. Much the same holds of our relation to nature, which is increasingly affected by human interven-tion. Tradition and nature were in the past like structuring landscapes of action. As things increasingly become non-natural and non-traditional, the more decisions have to be taken about them – by someone, not necessarily those most directly involved.

Consider human reproduction. Many aspects of reproduc-tion that used to be 'given' both by tradition and by the limits of nature are now in principle open to decisions, including not just whether you want a child or not, but what the sex of that child is going to be. Once these events are taken out of nature a whole series of risk-infused decisions has to be taken. We break away progressively from tradition and nature as risk becomes an organizing notion for all sorts of decisions that have to be taken politically and personally. Health is a good example. Health systems in the past tended to depend upon a notion of what I call 'external risk' – you get ill and the National Health Service takes care of you. But in a more saturated information environment, in which everybody to some extent is in contact with the findings of science and technology in relation to health, things are different. Whether on a conscious level or not, we are deciding across a multiplicity of alternatives. Every time we eat or drink, we make these kinds of decision. Contrary to what might be assumed, this situation cuts across all classes. It's not true that the world is more risky than it used to be. Rather the notion of risk becomes more central, as does trust because of the existence of more active trust systems.

Didn't premodern populations face risk? Couldn't we think of deteriorating circumstances in which fourteenth-century peasants, for example, might face a heightened risk of tuberculosis?

This is all to do with the difference between risk and danger or hazard mentioned earlier. Dangers and hazards have, of course, always existed. Life in the Middle Ages, for instance, was a perilous affair. In those days, however, people didn't think in terms of risk but much more in terms of fate or God-given fortune and misfortune.

To what extent is the sense of risk becoming heightened? As you suggest, we all have to make more decisions, but what we once thought was a question of calculability now often appears to us as a problem of incalculability. Knowledge seems to have carried us from the point where we had a positive belief that we could estimate what was the extent of the risk we faced (and could make

appropriate provision); we now have to acknowledge that we don't
actually know in any very useful way what are the chances of our
facing a given level of risk.

I deal with this in terms of a distinction I mentioned earlier.
Until relatively recently, many spheres of social life were dominated by 'external risks' – risks which are fairly well calculable on the basis of time-series. One measure of this is the
calculations of insurance companies, which assume a relative stability of lifestyle and a stability in nature, based as
they are on actuarial calculations. The very notion of insurance, as I mentioned earlier, goes along with the concept of a
calculable future, subject to human intervention. There are
still countries in the world today where you can't get insured
for items which in the West we take for granted (from health
care to baggage loss). Mishaps which befall people are often
assumed to be hazards of fate in more traditional cultures.
The idea that you can control hazard and therefore can be
insured against it – the rise of the notion of humanly engi-
neered safety – is part and parcel of Enlightenment thought.
What we are finding now is that the world isn't quite as the
Enlightenment thinkers assumed. Increasing our knowledge
about the world, the drive to produce information, create
new forms of risk for which we have little prior historical
experience – and which can't be calculated on the basis of
established time-series, for the data don't exist. Risk in financial markets is also problematic and complicated, because
it becomes more reflexive. In the electronic global market
place everyone has access to the same information as everyone else – everyone is guessing the guesses of others, who
are also guessing their guesses.
   What I call 'manufactured risk', or manufactured uncertainty, is bound up more with the advance of knowledge than

with its limitations. The economist Frank Knight (also a translator of Weber) made the distinction between risk and uncertainty. He argued that risk concerns future probabilities which can be calculated, uncertainty ones which cannot be. But that distinction doesn't hold water: there are too many fuzzy areas in the middle. There isn't a tight distinction between risk and uncertainty. Manufactured risk is risk, but of a new type.

Manufactured risk isn't associated only with human intervention in nature, but also with social change in an information society based upon high reflexivity. Consider marriage and the family, for example. Up to even a generation ago, marriage was structured by established traditions. When people got married, they knew, as it were, what they were doing. Marriage was formed to a large degree in terms of traditional expectations of gender, sexuality and so forth. Now it is a much more open system with new forms of risk. Everyone who gets married is conscious of the fact that divorce rates are high, that women demand greater equality than in the past. The very decision to get married is constitutively different from before. There has never been a high-divorce, high-remarriage society before. No one knows, for example, what its consequences are for the future of the family or for the health of children.

What's the nature of the interaction between new forms of risk and the growing domain of things that are 'insurable'?

There is a double process of change. On the one hand, there are more things you can insure against now than you could in the past – what began with Betty Grable's legs has become even more pervasive. One should even see derivatives markets as a kind of insurance: they are an attempt to lay off risk, so that now you can insure almost anything at an indefinite point of future time. That is very interesting. There is an extension of insurance at the same time as an alteration in its mechanisms. On the other hand, insurance companies are retreating from some of the risks they used happily to cover, including some forms of natural hazard – which, as they are very well aware, may not be 'natural' any longer. Companies are now very worried, for example, about catastrophe insurance. The welfare state, or at least its social security systems, could be seen as a giant insurance company, and it is also affected by shifting patterns of risk.

I think I can see the distinction between risk in a modern and premodern environment, but aren't many of the problems of the welfare state, for example, to be explained in terms of other causes: changing bases of political support, changing competence of the state, demographic change? For example, dependency ratios between older people who would formerly have been dependent on the welfare state and those who are active in the economy are becoming much less favourable.

There are of course more older people, but so far as welfare problems go it's not just the existence of more older people which is at issue, but the changing nature of old age as well – and this is strongly influenced by the transformations I've described. Old age itself is becoming deinstitutionalized and taken out of nature. Ageing is becoming more active and reflexive. Some of the physical illnesses or limitations once assumed to be linked to old age are governed largely by prior lifestyle habits. Older people should no longer be 'socially disqualified' at a certain age. That's why I don't like the idea of a pension, or that disabling term 'pensioner'. It seems to me a form of welfare dependency.

. . . but within the prevailing system there is still a period in which you are supposed not to work any more, that's a part of employment societies and the way that they are organized . . .

That's bound to change, I think.

Well, it's changing, but I guess that people will still tend to live beyond the time in which they are in gainful employment and that time is probably going to get longer. The retirement age will rise, but probably not in a way which will outweigh the increase in life expectancy.

No, I'm sure retirement will be abolished as a notion within a relatively short time, as is already happening in the US. There will be more mobility in and out of the labour force at different ages and people will have all sorts of different relationships to work. Old age is very much bound up with issues of risk and trust. It used to be more of a status passage. It's much less that now; older people have much the same opportunities and the same struggles as younger people. They get remarried, they have sexual lives, they face the question of 'what to tell the grandchildren'.

You identify a whole set of areas in which people have both sexual and pro-creative choices that previously didn't exist. There are new things that people have to make decisions about . . .

Well, it's not only that there are choices, but that choices *must* be made. That is, made by someone. Obviously there are strong elements of class division in all this, and differential power.

I wanted to ask you a further question about trust. Initially, trust seems a rather old idea and in older societies it often had a religious connotation (as in 'in God we trust'). What aspects of this remain today?

Trust originally becomes generalized from some of the same contexts as risk, in commercial relationships. Its religious sources are less important. The noun form of trust comes from that source as well, as when you talk about a bank as a trust, or holding things in trust and so on. If you think of trust as something relevant to the future rather than to the past, that's the basic difference. Previous forms of trust were much more deeply involved with more traditional forms of commitment and morality, such as kinship obligations. Trust involves a more directly future-oriented relationship with whomever or whatever you are trusting.

Trust has been described as involving faith rather than a calculated expectation. You don't trust somebody because of a rational calculation of the likelihood of his or her doing what he or she has promised but because you have a generalized faith in the capacity of a system or an individual to deliver. In some ways, faith perhaps rather consciously evokes a non-modern set of ideas.

No, it doesn't mean faith in that sense, it relates back more to the theme of security. This is what commercial trusts provide, for example – financial security. Much the same is true of trust in personal relationships too. Trust has to be mutual to be effective, and it offers security in the face of future contingencies. That's why I relate it to the idea of basic security in personality, as well.

But is it not still faith as a non-rational commitment?

Partly non-rational, certainly – or a preparedness to accept the security that others can offer. To survive in life at all you need a generalized notion of trust, and that's essentially something people get from their early emotional experiences. If you don't have that, you're in big trouble. But to repeat, to be effective trust is always reciprocal – it never rests upon blind faith.

But isn't it the case that we have conventional or 'rule of thumb' ways of making assessments, which are not simply acts of faith? Take the example of flying. Most of us know that most planes most of the time get to their destination. One way of knowing that the pilot is competent is that you know every time Qantas has flown this route previously, the passengers have got through. We don't have to know how the plane works.

That's why I say that trust is not so different from risk. It's obviously not purely an emotional commitment. There's always some kind of calculative basis to trust, and you're not going to trust another person unless you get some kind of evidence of her or his trustworthiness. The same applies to trust in expert systems, like airways, whose security is after all bolstered by a variety of professional procedures and checks. In the example of the plane, you are making a risk assessment, aren't you?

If you think about it, as I think you believe that people do.

Well, they often do on the level of practical consciousness. Those who discuss risk often underestimate people's rationality. I don't think that it is particularly stupid to have a fear of flying, for example, and still drive a car. Risk presumes a set of values and the thing that might upset you most about planes, for instance, is that you have absolutely no control over what happens in them.

I guess that one of the reasons for saying that trust has this in-creased prominence under modernity is because there are so many more encounters and situations in which we are not in control or in which we are dealing with unfamiliar people. If you take travel as an example, in a premodern society you might expect that a peasant might never get further than the pub on the edge of the village. And he would walk there. To get here today, I have trav-elled down on the train under one expert system, then through the Underground on another. It just seems that there are many more contexts in a modern society where you might have to exer-cise trust.

This is definitely so – and confront risks, because of the much more open character of experience. Notions of fate, even pro-pitiation, don't disappear altogether. Even in wholly secularized contexts, superstitions persist. They might be followed in an embarrassed way, but they have a remnant of the charms and sacrifices of previous ages.

There's a further issue I would like to raise about expertise, ex-pert knowledge and the knowledgeability of actors.

The rise of expertise is a key part of modernity as well. There is a difference between expertise and the traditional claims to knowledge of religious officials, witch doctors, spiritual lead-ers or whatever, because expertise depends upon knowledge which, in principle, anyone could acquire, and without hav-ing to perform specialized, arcane rituals to do so. So we are all experts in some aspects of our lives these days.

Well, that's one of the issues I wanted to raise. In some ways, you might say that expertise precisely does involve arcane rituals, and if you think of it in terms of the sociology of the professions, expert knowledge systems tend to be marked off, they have a particular code, creed, forms of interaction, their own jargon and those kinds of thing which in some sense protect these practices and do mystify those forms of knowledge.

Let me take a particular example of the difficulty with expert systems, one which relates to issues of nuclear power (and about which you have written). There is a very vigorous disagreement amongst 'experts' about whether nuclear power generation is actually an extremely environmentally damaging technology, or the only way of producing clean fuel. Now perhaps the weight of informed opinion appears to be concentrated at one pole or the other. But the problem for a lay person is that she or he has no way of making a judgement about who is right, and the fact that one of these opinions might have a great weight of authority behind it isn't of much value in reaching such a judgement.

That seems to me just characteristic of our situation of dependence on expertise; I don't think it's specific to nuclear power. It's true much more generically that there is no authority of all authorities to turn to, so that we are all simultaneously both experts and lay people in different areas of our lives. That brings us back again to trust and risk, because at a certain point one just has to make a decision, or perhaps decide not to make a decision, but without any ultimate authority to turn to. It's quite hard to live like that, but that is how we have to live.

It's just that nuclear power is a particularly significant and consequential example, and one which illustrates very clearly the issues around expert systems.

It illustrates important aspects of what it's like to live in a world of multiple expertise, with multiple claims to authority.

Again, that's bound up with our release, if that's what it is, from tradition and nature. And it's become highly generalized. We should think about expertise not just in relation to the usual areas, but also in relation to activities like counselling, for example. Personal life is also invaded by expertise and there one finds exactly the same dilemmas. Open the Yellow Pages under psychotherapy and you find fifty different kinds of therapist advertised there. Who can say which you should call? And who can advise you whether or not therapy as such is complete nonsense? Only experts themselves: but they often disagree, or there wouldn't be fifty kinds of therapy in the first place. There are settings in which findings or evidence will be pretty well conclusive, and where experts will speak with one voice. But there are many situations where they don't, and I find this in even the most mundane things of life. Every plumber who comes to fix anything always says of his predecessor 'How did anyone ever fix the pipes in such a way, what did they think they were doing?'

But in these examples, judgements are much easier for a lay person to make. If your plumber says he has done a terrific job but the taps don't run or the water is always cold, you have some reason to think that he hasn't done a terrific job. Nuclear power is much more difficult both because of the complexity and the scale, and because of the questions of when you would know and how you would know which expert claims were right.

Yes, although there's no clear break between the two examples. There are very many others like the instance of nuclear power – these are the complexities of late modernity. When there isn't an expert consensus, there are always problems about the dissemination of knowledge claims into the public realm. For example, in the case of BSE the conventional left-of-centre explanation is that the problem arose from a lack of regulation in the food industry, and the whole thing should have come to public awareness earlier than it did. But the origins of BSE lie less in inadequate regulation than in the break away from nature that I mentioned earlier. And the public announcement of such risks is itself a risky affair, with no absolute guidelines. The statement about BSE and humans proved to be very consequential for the economy and the beef industry. On the other hand, not making such a statement at the time when it was made would have been equally dubious. This is a dilemma between being accused of scaremongering on the one hand and cover-ups on the other. Given the controversial nature of such risk situations, I don't see any clear strategy for dealing with this. It's going to be very difficult for governments and for businesses in a world of high technological change, knowing what to say to whom, how and when.

Following on from this, is it true to say that in late modernity knowledge is more commodified, that knowledge production and dissemination are more under the guidance of commercial imperatives and interests?

Obviously it is true to some degree. There are very strong market imperatives, but science has become globalized, open-ended and essentially uncontrollable. It's not simply carried on at the whim of commercial interests, and no one knows where scientific and technological innovations will lead.

I'm just thinking in terms of lay actors' evaluation of and trust in accounts they are given. One of the things that lay actors look to is to see, crudely, who's paying this guy to say or do all these kinds of thing. If you are on the payroll of Philip Morris, for example, and you come out and say there is no proof of an associa-

tion between smoking and lung cancer, people might be more scep-
tical than if you were working, for example, for the Medical Re-
search Council.

Those would be relevant considerations. But there are more general issues about the impact of expertise and claims to knowledge. For example, a commercial organization might set a group of scientists a particular task, to produce some result, but they don't and can't consider all the outcomes it might have – as with the genetic modification of food. No one knows what medium- or longer-term consequences there might be, because they can't be tested in advance. BSE is a type-case for these issues. Nobody knows how serious or otherwise the spread of the illness might be. We are surrounded by areas where we don't really know what we have done to the existing order of things and what the consequences will be.

You seem to suggest – here and elsewhere – that there is a height-
ened and generalized sense of anxiety in living under late moder-
nity.

I don't think that. There are just different sources of anxiety. In the Middle Ages, there was plenty to be worried about, as we mentioned earlier. It's just that now the sources of anxiety are bound up with what we have done to the world rather than what God might do to it or to us.

But you have suggested that there are aspects of the things that
should make us anxious in late modernity which are qualitatively
different – nuclear weaponry is one and the threat to the entire
global infrastructure is another – so that we are now at least
potentially anxious about things which are perhaps even more

cataclysmic than the things that confronted people in previous ages. And also we have some sense of there being a scientifically discernible risk of these things happening, of possibilities which are very remote but extraordinarily catastrophic, that might be enough to encourage people under late modernity to be more anxious than their forebears.

I rather doubt that. There certainly are high-consequence risks that we have ourselves created. Since we recognize that we have created them, they are different from the fear of God in previous ages, or other forms of cataclysm attributed to demons and spirits. There are plenty of forms of insecurity around and many of these are different from those of previous ages, but I don't think one could say much beyond that.

One thing we have not discussed very explicitly in talking about modernity is the idea of reflexivity, an idea which you suggest is extremely important and actually goes back to the things you were saying about knowledgeable actors, practical consciousness and so on.

It also relates to all the things we are talking about. Reflexivity has two senses, one very general, and the other more directly relevant to modern social life. All human beings are reflective in the sense in which thinking about what one does is part of doing it, whether consciously or on the level of practical consciousness. Social reflexivity refers to a world increasingly constituted by information rather than pre-given modes of conduct. It is how we live after the retreat of tradition and nature, because of having to take so many forward-oriented decisions. In that sense, we live in a much more reflexive way than previous generations have done.

I think there is perhaps a contrast between what you say in The Consequences of Modernity *and what the German social theorist Ulrich Beck says in* The Reinvention of Politics. *Beck has a periodization between simple modernization and a reflexive kind of modernization. Do you believe that we have moved through modernity from a 'simple' to a more 'reflexive' mode?*

Yes, although the division isn't clear cut. Reflexive modernization says something about late modernity, reflecting on the limitations and difficulties of modernity itself. That relates to key problems of modern politics, because simple or linear modernization still predominates in some parts of the world, most notably in South-East Asia, at least up until recently. In the West and the developed industrial societies, there are conditions of reflexive modernization, with the key problem of modernization being what modernization itself is all about.

You talk sometimes as well of the more recent period as 'radicalized' modernity. How radicalized?

Well, it's just the same thing really: the increasing erosion of tradition and nature. The radicalization of modernity means being forced to live in a more reflexive way, facing a more open and problematic future.

Some people have concluded that this process of the transformation of modernity is actually delivering us into something else which is post-modern. *You seem to resist that judgement.*

Yes. What other people call post-modern I think of as the radicalizing of modernity in the sense in which we have discussed it. The dynamic sources of modernity are still there: the expansion of capitalism, the transformative effects of science and technology, the expansion of mass democracy. So I prefer to speak of reflexive modernization rather than post-modernity. There is only modernity and we can only reflect on modernity through modernity; that means also through science and technology. There is no escape from science and technology except through science and technology.

One way of describing the Enlightenment is in terms of the 'dare to know' motif. In some ways, you appear to argue that at one time the commitment to science and knowledge led to more positive expectations: the view that we could control and transform the world through knowledge. But also within this commitment lies the sense that if you really dare to know, you end up knowing that you don't know that much, or that there is not that much you can know with any kind of certainty. It seems to me that you want to roll both of these kinds of knowing into modernity. Don't post-modernists have a case when they say that the first of these ways of knowing – the expectation of control and the plasticity of the world to knowledge – is distinctive from the second and much more doubtful, uncertain side of daring to know?

I'm not sure this would be the main distinction involved with the notion of post-modernity as ordinarily understood. It is more accurate to say that we are experiencing a renewed encounter with science and technology. For a long while, science and technology were more insulated from everyday life than they are now. Today scientific findings and technological change impact upon us in an immediate way – we have a more dialogic or interrogatory relation with them than in the past. We are all finding out what philosophers of science have uncovered, that science rests upon organized scepticism – a preparedness to give up even cherished beliefs; upon contestation and the mutual critique of scientific experts.

Interview Five

From the Transformation of Intimacy to Life Politics

CHRISTOPHER PIERSON   *You have suggested that modernity or late modernity operates in two ways: in a very extensive mode as globalization (which you have talked about previously) but also in a very intensive and personalized one too. You have also talked about the way in which modernity changes the nature of the intimate and the personal. I wonder if you could say something about these ways in which modernity transforms self-identity.*

ANTHONY GIDDENS   To respond to that we need to pursue further the issue of the changing state of tradition, custom and habit. Modernity always set itself against tradition, but in many areas of life, tradition persisted – particularly in everyday life. The reason was primarily the dominant position of the patriarchal family, which remained undemocratized. That family form, together with the norms of gender and sexuality associated with it, is now breaking down, creating both opportunities and dilemmas in its wake.

   The changes involved here signal not just the transformation of intimacy but in a way the creation of intimacy. The rhetoric of intimacy is relatively new; it reflects a post-traditional world where emotional communication becomes crucial to the sustaining of relationships inside and outside of marriage. The patriarchal family of course reflected men's economic dominance, but its emotional inequalities seem to me equally important. It allocated a central role to male sexuality, linking virtuous women to marriage, separating them from the various categories of fallen women – prostitutes, courtesans and harlots. That schismatic view of women still persists, among both sexes, but it is manifestly incompatible with relationships formed through equal communication. Where achievable, 'intimacy' implies equality, in (what are now called) relationships, a word that is also relatively new, as used in this cluster of intimacy-type notions and actions.

All this is the other pole of globalization, where globalization means not just economic but wider structural and institutional change, having a profound impact on day-to-day life. The debate about the 'traditional family' has to be put in this context. Some social critics think we should try to return to this family form. In so far as there was a single traditional family (which we know there wasn't!) it was patriarchal, based on the aforementioned emotional schism between male and female sexuality, and on an authority system where children had few rights. The changes which have happened in these areas are part and parcel of processes of democratization in personal life – where for the first time men and women in principle treat one another as equals, and where children have rights. At the same time, extraordinary things are being revealed about the dark side of the 'traditional family', its unpleasant and exploitative aspects. If these are put alongside evidence about the conduct of some (no doubt a minority) of the most respected figures in the community, like priests, traditional family institutions look less than wholly appealing.

2. The incipient democratization of the private sphere has its crisis aspects, especially around divorce and fatherless children, but these changes are themselves global and I can't see any society that's going to escape them.

Is the change actually in the way that people experience their lives or is it a change in terms of disclosure, of publicity, particularly in terms of practices?

It's both – the one goes along with the other. To be in a relationship, married or not, means opening oneself up to the other. Relationships generate and sustain trust through disclosure. It's not enough just to say 'you're a wife and I'm a husband and this defines our roles'. Intimacy has its own contradictions and its problems. Wherever tradition and custom decline, the possibility of obsession arises – and this applies in the sphere of relationships too. The idea of co-dependency is interesting here – the mutually compulsive nature of certain kinds of relationship. Co-dependency is a way of thinking about people locked into compulsive relationships. It's a way of life, not a very satisfactory one; it's the opposite of a good relationship, based upon trust in and commitment to the other.

These changes – and their problematic aspects – have their parallels in apparently quite different spheres. Consider recent changes in the nature of management. Twenty years ago, management was normally thought of as a static term, *the* management. Now management is managing – an active endeavour, at which both sides have to work. There's a similar story about networking, because networking is a way of actively sustaining connections in a detraditionalizing society. To some extent one can still rely upon established roles, but networking means forming relationships with other people in an active and open way – it involves what I call active trust, as in many other sectors of social life today. Networking is quite egalitarian and it invokes the rhetoric of intimacy, even if it is clearly distinct from friendship. It's striking how many people use first names quickly now, compared to even a few years ago. This is a 'stripped-down' version of intimacy, because everybody knows that, like gift-making, there is a sort of deception hidden in it. A person is friendly with others but at the same time everyone accepts that there is a subtext to it all – that useful connections are being forged. A lot of business is now done that way and a lot of academic life is done that way too.

I guess some people would say that the down-side of that relationship is that, to some extent, real intimacy or friendship is in danger of being commodified. Not only do the people who work together speak on first-name terms but also people who 'cold call' you to buy their replacement windows insist on using first-name terms.

That's more a case of people exploiting what's essentially a relatively egalitarian relationship. People usually only network with those they define as relative equals anyway. This doesn't necessarily create egalitarianism, but it does depend upon a presumption of equality – upon a tacit understanding that there are limits to what one can do and expect from other people. I used books on self-help as a research resource to explore intimacy (in *The Transformation of Intimacy*). I've recently been doing the same for networking. One of the principles of networking, these books say, is that it's not whom you know, it's who knows you. What the individual is trying to do is to make himself or herself visible in a network of people who may be able to help and whom that person might be able to help. In the higher circles of power, it is like the old power élite but much more actively organized – it has to be constantly worked at, like intimate relationships.

The transformation of intimacy probably applies most profoundly in the area of gender. To what extent do you see that process driven by a willed political movement, and to what extent are the changes a by-product of bigger, globalizing social processes?

I see them as connected. For example, the women's movement in its modern form wouldn't have been possible without the structural changes altering the nature of the labour force, propelling more women into the labour force, the changes in pre-existing family forms and so forth. The women's movement self-consciously built upon, and contributed to, these trends. Activists within the women's movement were well aware of such structural changes and indeed were the first to analyse them effectively. But consequences followed that no one fully anticipated, including the sheer rapidity in the changes in women's position as measured in historical time. Not long ago, many said 'we are dealing with thousands of years of history here: how could that be changed quickly?' But the position of men and women has changed in a relatively short time.

You suggest that there are surprisingly rapid changes in this area. I want to ask you how much has really changed. To what extent are love, sex, relationships wholly different for late moderns? And to what extent do old vices lurk beneath new forms?

I think there are big changes. People who say they want a return to the traditional family plainly accept that there have been, or they wouldn't be saying what a crisis there is. But as you imply, a good deal of the old hangs around in the new. Take for example the issue of male sexual violence against women. In premodern and early modern times, men policed women's sexuality. They did so not just by controlling women directly, but by male-on-male sanctions, including the use of violence. Thus they defended the division between the 'virtuous' woman and the 'fallen' woman. Men can no longer police women's sexuality in this way. It's possible that a good deal of violence from men towards women now isn't just the persistence of the old system, but an inability or unwillingness to adapt to the new. That is, it isn't just the continuation of traditional patriarchy, but a response to its crumbling.

I see the current situation more positively than some critics do, partly because aspects of the patriarchal family, including such policing, were outrageous by current standards. At the same time, what is going on is an adventure; we don't know how all this will come out. It goes along with changes in the role of children too, particularly the emergence of the 'prized child'. Virtually no one has children for economic reasons any more in Western countries – the cost of having a child in the UK is £50,000 over that child's lifetime. Once children start to have a semi-mythical status, the surrounding ethos about parenting and protection of children and so forth shifts. What we would regard as maltreatment of children was surprisingly common in the past, including culturally sanctioned infanticide. To us the killing of an infant is a gigantic crime. It's good that children have rights, that people now prize children, and that most don't have children without thinking about it quite a lot beforehand. These are all aspects of democratization, whatever further problems and anxieties they might bring in their wake.

We have had a recent history of very high-profile cases of child abuse. We don't really know if there are new forms and levels of abuse or simply an unmasking of things that have always gone on. Isn't it very hard to make a judgement about what is new and what is increased disclosure or a new kind of sensibility?

It's very difficult in the case of (what we now regard as) child abuse. Probably there always was at least as high a level of such abuse, including sexual abuse, as nowadays. It's easy to see how such practices could be passed across the generations. But we'll never know.

I'll put one last prompt in that area. You talk about pure relation-ships *as a kind of characteristic of this period, and I guess the sceptic might ask just how 'pure' in your sense our relationships have become. A lot of people might accept that there have been some very substantive changes, but there are lots of women who still find themselves in relationships for material or economic rea-sons. For many of them, the choice is still very strongly delim-ited.*

There is obviously a strong class factor, as there is in this whole area of the changing nature of tradition and custom. That af-fects the sphere of personal relations as much as any other.

To what extent are pure relationships 'pure', then?

Well, they are actually pretty impure! What we have is a strong tendency towards relationships based upon emotional com-munication rather than institutionally given gender roles – in relations between men and women, between same-sex part-ners, and also between parents and children. But there are many situations where there are still traditional family forms and the persistence of old attitudes. The idea of the pure rela-tionship is an ideal type – there is a mixed situation on the

ground. Nevertheless, to repeat, these are large changes. Most
of us, affluent and poor alike, are struggling with them, without as yet a clear institutional outcome. There aren't as clear
institutional supports and frameworks for democratizing personal life as there are in the case of the public sphere.

*Can I just ask you one question about the way you describe this
process as democratization or personal democracy or 'intimacy
as democracy'. Why do you describe this process as 'democratization'?*

Because it does closely track the ideals of public democracy.
When I was working on *The Transformation of Intimacy*, I put
David Held's book *Models of Democracy* alongside a typical
self-help text on intimacy. It is striking how far norms of formal democracy, as Held describes them, resemble those of a
good relationship. Democracy means recognizing that all people are equal: each has a vote and no one's vote counts more
than any other. In a democracy, political life is founded on
dialogue rather than on violence or coercion – or tradition.
Issues, in principle anyway, are publicly discussed and an attempt to reach consensus made.

   A good relationship is also one in which each party is equal
and autonomous, in which issues are discussed rather than
driven underground, and which is free from violence. Communication has a key role in public democracy and in relationships. If there is no space in a relationship where the parties
can actually talk to one another, the relationship tends to become obsessive, or it sinks into some habitual structure. Communication means being capable of disclosure and being
able to talk when necessary. It would be stupid to say, either
in democracy or in a good relationship, that we should be
talking all the time, because it would drive us mad! But in

both, there's the chance of influencing the behaviour of other people without using force or invoking the power of tradition.

Isn't it really just the case that good democratic practices and good personal relationships share in what David Held calls the 'principle of autonomy'? A political scientist thinking about democracy is likely to think of things like the rule of law, transparent procedures and so on. Proper procedures and law-like relationships are not what you'd expect to see in good intimate relations. Good personal relationships don't normally come down to a vote!

Well, nor does good democracy! For the most part, if a political system is working well people trust political leaders and let them get on with it, as Max Weber said. But they can get rid of their leaders if they want to. Thus a core principle of democratic personal relationships is the possibility of divorce or separation. In traditional families, women were chattels – possessions – of their husbands in law, and in practice, for economic reasons too, had little chance of quitting a marriage. As regards the law, the connection between public and personal democracy here is close because of the centrality of legal rights and obligations in both.

I don't see all this as leading simply and inevitably to a happier life. Things are more complex than that. Democracy in the public sphere has its problems and weaknesses – it isn't a panacea for all social difficulties. Much the same is true of the democratizing of personal life. Not only do pre-established attitudes towards gender and sexuality persist, the pure relationship has its own contradictions. For example, if you commit yourself to someone and you're very open with him or her, it can also give him or her power over you if he or she should choose to exploit it. In anything close to a pure relationship, one is always on the line in some sense.

Well, people don't want to reproblematize their relationships every morning when they get up!

Of course not. That's why trust is so important in a happy relationship – but nowadays this has to be active trust, rather than dependence upon institutionalized roles.

This raises, in a particular instance, something more general about the way you treat modernity and late modernity. Some processes you identify seem to refer to modernity as distinctive from traditional society. In other instances, you seem to suggest that actually late modernity is the reversal of things that have gone on elsewhere and earlier in modernity. Do you think the crucial break is the coming of late modernity, or is the crucial break the division between traditional and modern society?

The most fundamental division is the earlier one, for sure. But there are very good reasons to be preoccupied with what is happening now. I think there is a new kind of capitalism, a new kind of economy, a new kind of global order, a new kind of personal life coming into being, all of which differ from earlier phases of social development.

I'd like to persist a bit with the theme of tradition and modernity, and later ask you to relate this back to our personal lifestyles. You talk a lot about the changes affecting tradition. Could you define tradition?

Tradition brings us back yet again to the theme of time. It is a means whereby the past lives in the present and thereby shapes the future. Traditions involve the following qualities: (1) they depend upon ritual, which often, although not always, takes the form of collective ceremonial; (2) they involve repetition and therefore a certain classicism; (3) they imply a notion of 'ritual truth'. The truth of tradition is given by the codes of practice which it enshrines. This is the crux of the differences between traditional ways of doing things and those based upon rational or scientific inquiry. Of course, particular kinds of activity or institution can involve elements of each: the practice of science, for example, can take on traditional traits. (4) Tradition is always collective: individuals can have their own rituals, but traditions as such are group properties. (5) The reason for this, as the French sociologist Maurice Halbwachs pointed out, is that tradition is a form of collective memory. It transmits experiences through ritual.

We have to avoid some of the misconceptions which surround the idea of tradition. It is a myth to suppose that traditions are unchanging. The best book on tradition, written by Edward Shils, makes it clear that traditions are not frozen. Change is normally evolutionary, because of the central importance of ritual and repetition. It is also wrong to suppose that, for a given type of behaviour to be traditional, it must have existed over very long periods of time – over hundreds of years. Traditional beliefs and practices of this sort do exist – the world's major religions have endured intact for thousands of years. However, tradition depends upon its ritual claim to truth and the ceremonial elements connected with this. Traditions can be invented and become stabilized in quite a short order of time.

The historian Eric Hobsbawm coined the phrase 'the invention of tradition' to refer to forms of ritual which were deliberately fostered by élite groups in the nineteenth century as part of their claims to power. Some of the trappings of royalty, for example, which we might assume go back for centuries, weren't established until the late nineteenth century. It is implied that they aren't authentic traditions because they are relatively recent and they were constructed in a deliberate way. I don't think this view is correct. Traditions have been invented and reinvented throughout history, with greater or lesser degrees of contrivance. Tradition is intimately bound up with power. For instance, Christian traditions mostly took it for granted that women would have little or no role in the public domain.

Finally, we should recognize that traditions are hardly ever unitary. Traditions lend themselves to different interpretations, even though all those involved may claim adherence to the same classical texts and indeed perhaps each claim to be the sole authentic interpreter of those texts.

You talk of the 'end of tradition' in contemporary society. But what does this actually mean? I can't see how tradition as you've described it could ever disappear, because it would seem to be so pervasive a feature of social life.

Just like 'the end of nature', the end of tradition doesn't mean that the world it describes disappears, but rather that its role in our lives becomes transformed. Traditional cultures, and traditional ways of doing things, persist all across the world, including within Western societies. The process of the invention and reinvention of tradition goes on. At the same time, largely as a result of intensifying globalization and reflexivity, in large areas of our lives what was tradition (and its less ritualized cousin, custom) is altered or destroyed. Tradition dissolves into kitsch, souvenirs and trinkets tourists buy in airport shops. Or else tradition becomes the heritage industry, within which one should include tourism itself. Heritage isn't tradition, since it lacks the core elements of collective involvement in ritual and repetition. It is tradition reduced to spectacle. Finally, in the current world tradition borders on a much more dangerous phenomenon – fundamentalism. Fundamentalism in my view is part of the fate of tradition in the late modern world.

Can you be more precise about what fundamentalism actually is, though? The word often seems to be used simply for the beliefs of groups one happens not to like. One person's fundamentalist is another's committed believer. Rather few of those whom others call 'fundamentalists' seem to accept the label as applying to themselves. Those involved with radical Islam, for example, don't accept the label at all.

I believe fundamentalism is a recent phenomenon. The word has only been in common coinage since the 1970s. Fundamentalism for me is tradition waging a bitter battle against a cosmopolitan, reflexive world which asks for reasons. It is more than a schism between different categories of true believer: it is a deliberate opting out of that 'cosmopolitan conversation of humankind' of which the American philosopher Richard Rorty speaks. Refusal of dialogue – an insistence that only one view of the world is possible and that one is already in possession of it – has a particular, and potentially destructive, significance in a world which precisely depends more and more upon it. Fundamentalism is a concept which only makes sense against the backdrop of late modernity, the generalizing and radicalizing of modern institutions.

It may be fuelled by the same emotions as fanaticism in previous ages, but it has a different significance for us and its content isn't the same. Fundamentalism is tradition which self-consciously sets itself against modernity, but which at the same time takes on modern qualities and quite often uses modern technologies. American religious fundamentalists were the first actively to use television as a means of promoting their doctrines.

Like ideology, fundamentalism doesn't refer to any particular beliefs or practices. Fundamentalism is the use of ritual truth to deny dialogue actively and therefore isn't limited to the area of religion. There can be, and are, fundamentalist forms of ethnicity, nationalism and politics. It isn't directly relevant whether or not a given group would accept the term fundamentalism. As with all sociological terms, it becomes part of the very struggles it describes.

You seem to treat fundamentalism as an enemy. Is there any positive side to it?

I do think combating fundamentalism should be a prime political goal. Fundamentalism is dangerous because it is always edged with the possibility of violence. All the way through from personal life to global systems, dialogue offers the possibility of replacing violence with communication. Our civilization now is intrinsically cosmopolitan. Fundamentalism threatens its very essence.

For the reasons I have given, fundamentalism has to be seen as something other than the clash of traditions. Fundamentalism isn't the same as simply resisting modernity and it certainly isn't the same as criticizing Westernization. For instance, Islamic movements and groups are often lumped together by Western observers as fundamentalist without discrimination. Like any world religion, Islam contains many different interpretations and viewpoints as well as of course common roots with Christianity.

Fundamentalism does have positive aspects, although in

my view these can't be retrieved unless we hold back from fundamentalism itself. Science and technology, the driving cultural forces of modernity, depend upon the presumption that 'nothing is sacred'. All beliefs and practices are in principle open to revision in the light of new knowledge. The fundamentalist questions that principle and is right to do so. For the idea that nothing is sacred, pushed to its extreme, is impossible to live with – there would be no moral order left in our lives. The problem for us – those who wish to see a cosmopolitan world prosper – is to reconcile commitment and scepticism. This isn't any longer an abstract question: we are already doing it in our everyday lives, and this new accommodation helps explain some features of what is happening to the sphere of personal relationships and intimacy.

Are there any contexts in which it is reasonable to defend tradition?

There are many. What we shouldn't attempt is to justify tradition in the traditional way, which is what fundamentalism seeks to do. If they are not to degenerate into the other forms I've mentioned, traditions have to be justified; yet in a way the whole point of tradition is that it carries its own justification through its claims to ritual truth. It might make sense in some circumstances to defend that. It might be argued that some of the rituals associated with Parliament, for example, should keep going. But this would be because they provide continuity and contribute to political legitimacy. Whichever way one looks at it, tradition can't be the same in a world based on discourse and the giving of reasons.

You relate the changed status of tradition in modern societies to the growth of compulsions and addictions. Why?

The issue of compulsiveness and the spread of the idea of addiction to me are extremely interesting. Compulsiveness was analysed by Freud in terms of obsession-compulsions – everyday habits that have compulsive aspects, such as someone who has to wash his hands forty times before he is sure they are clean. Obsession-compulsions still exist, but today compulsiveness has become much more generalized in its significance. Consider the history of addiction. The idea of 'an addict' was unknown in the nineteenth century. 'Addiction' was first of all used to refer to alcohol addiction and what has come to be called 'drug addiction'. These things didn't happen until well into the current century. Alcohol had long been considered a problem by the public authorities, but mainly in relation to drunkenness and social disorder. The idea of 'the alcoholic', involving a medicalized terminology of addiction, didn't exist at that point – 'the drunk' was a different type of figure.

What interests me particularly is the spread of the notion of addiction well beyond the original spheres of alcohol and drugs. These days one can be said to be addicted to anything, from work, exercise or eating through to relationships, sexuality and even love. Is this simply the spread of the concept, or are we becoming more of an addictive society?

I think both are true and one can explain them by reference to the changes we have been discussing. Consider, for instance, sexual addiction. On the face of it such a notion seems rather absurd, because couldn't one argue that sex is a driving force of human life in any case – how could the idea of addiction have any purchase here? It can and does if we recognize that to speak of addiction is to speak of compulsiveness. The man who phones sex call lines several times a day, feels disgusted with himself each time, but can't stop is plainly caught up in a cycle of sexual compulsion. All addictions have a similar character. They begin with a source of pleasure, whether this be the buzz someone gets from a successful piece of work, from running in the mornings, from food or sex. That pleasure becomes part of an addictive cycle when it comes to be a fix – when the source of pleasure becomes a high, from which the pleasure element itself actually recedes. Many addictive cycles are degenerative: the individual can't live without the regular fix, the intervals between them become shorter and the level of anxiety higher.

Compulsiveness is for us one of the prime enemies of the good life. I explain it as the other side of the retreat of tradition. Compulsiveness can invade any context of life from which tradition has been evacuated. In all such contexts there is a tension between increased autonomy on the one hand and compulsiveness on the other. Like tradition, addiction is involved with the hold of the past over the present. Rather than this being ritual, moral and collective, in the case of addiction it is personal and driven by anxiety and insecurity.

Like tradition, addictions are marked by ritual and repetition. Perhaps one could say they are the personal and emotional expression of the dictum that 'those who do not understand the past are compelled to repeat it'. Anyone in the thrall of an addiction is no longer the master of his or her individual life and has sacrificed exactly those qualities of increased autonomy which represent one of the major gains of detraditionalization. The problem for all of us today is to establish relatively stable lifestyle habits which, however, don't slip too far into compulsiveness. For no one could carry reflexivity too far – everyday life is built around consistency of habit or custom and therefore repetition. Most people today have some compulsive elements to their lives, whether this be in the area of work or elsewhere.

How far can one generalize this, though, to the society or culture as a whole?

I believe we do now live in a society scarred by compulsiveness. The furthering of individual autonomy and self-esteem in everyday life should be regarded as just as important a political task as legal and other freedoms in the public sphere. These are to an extent the condition of those freedoms.

As seems to me the case with some other topics we've talked about, I wonder whether you are treating as new elements of the social and personal which have always existed? You say that intimacy is a recent invention in history. Surely, if intimacy means close communication and trust, it has existed whenever individuals have formed close relationships in marriage and other spheres?

No, the present-day situation is different from the past, even the relatively recent past, in several distinct ways, although of course there are continuities too.

First, relationships have to be made and sustained much more actively than was the case three or four decades ago, let alone in previous periods of history. This is again connected to the changed character of tradition and the rise of social reflexivity. Consider friendship, for example. Friendship relations in the past have often effectively been forms of comradeship: people have a close emotional understanding of one another because of sharing common life experiences. Many men's friendships have been and are like this. They come from having been at the same school, in the army together and so forth. Self-revelation wasn't the basis of such friendships, so much as communality of experience.

Second, in the areas of marriage and the family we now live

in a society in which for the first time not just men and women, but men, women and children, are equals before the law – and are much more equal on a substantial level than formerly was the case. Relations between equals, as I mentioned in the instance of networking, have to be negotiated. They depend upon active trust.

Third, many contemporary relationships are formed largely through dialogue; they have no other anchor. Take the example of marriage, which for generations was above all an economic affair and was treated as almost like a state of nature. Either one was married or one was not. How well a person got on with his or her spouse was certainly important for whether or not the marriage was happy, but was not the basis of marriage itself. Now, by and large, it is. (Many more conservative cultural critics find this disturbing.)

Fourth, there is the rise, and today more or less universal hold, of values of romantic love. Sexual love always existed, but both the idea of 'romance' and its tie to marriage are developments which stretch back only about a century. Romantic love is all about emotional communication and the specialness of the other. Romantic love carries with it the idea of intimacy because one falls in love specifically with the qualities of the other. Love here has no connotation of obligation or duty, although of course these can be built around it. Romance also involves a personalized narrative, a storyline which the individual in love develops about himself or herself and the other. Romantic love has in fact a double relation to intimacy. In so far as it is relatively immediate, a bolt from the blue, romantic love is obviously a projection and one marked, as Freud observed, by infantile qualities. The ideals of romantic love stand at odds with intimacy based upon a full understanding of the good and the not-so-good qualities of the other.

Some have questioned the notion that romantic love is a specifi-cally Western ideal, claiming to find similar notions and values in prior periods of European history as well as in other cultures. What is the nature of romantic love and is it as specifically bound up with the modern period as you claim?

I don't know of a comparative anthropology of love, so no one would be in a fully informed position to answer that question. What we do know is that there are many cultures, and historical periods, which have been studied in detail and where the ideals of romantic love are unknown. Romantic love, as I mentioned, isn't the same as sexual love or what used to be called in the Middle Ages *amor passion*. Love in the sense of sexual passion conjoined to devotion to and adoration of another is a commonplace feature of all societies. Of course, those kinds of feeling were virtually never made the prime basis of marriage, which in all cultures until recently was a matter of economics, inheritance and the formation of kinship alliances. *Amor passion* was nearly always regarded as unstable and indeed is unstable, because sexual attraction can easily fade or be transferred and emotional identification can also rapidly shift.

Romantic love invokes similar feelings, but makes of them something quite different. *Amor passion* is usually described in stories as flouting orthodox conventions and as a specifically disruptive force – thus most stories about it in more traditional cultures end in tragedy, since the lovers are doomed. The same motif surfaces in early accounts of romantic love, which is why one of its main interpreters, Denis de Rougement, associates romantic love with an absorption with death. I don't think he is right. Courtly love, on which he focused his attention, wasn't in fact the true origin of notions of romantic love, although some elements appear there. The idea of romantic love only really develops in the late eighteenth century and reflects a wider concern with narrative form expressed also in the rise of the novel. Romantic love tells a story, it depends upon a narrative, but this is a forward-looking one. On the level of personal life, it meshes with the characteristic orientation of modernity towards colonizing an 'empty' future.

Romantic love essentially creates a biography, not just for one person but for two. It is a moral and emotional complex which helps create the *couple*, which when we move forward to our times has effectively replaced marriage, or is what marriage has become. Most forms of traditional marriage were based not on the couple, but upon the connections of husband and wife with other kin, especially children. This went along, obviously, with a pronounced sexual division of labour. For us, the couple takes primacy even over children and of course is a system of sexual and emotional communication rather than an economic unit. We take the world of coupledom for granted, but it is an extraordinary phenomenon. To be in a couple is to be in a relationship that creates its own history which is personalized and may have little connection with the wider society. The world of coupledom is exclusionary: it is the contemporary form of the division between the married and unmarried, but with quite a different character. It goes along with a society in which many people, at least for substantial periods, live on their own, but at any point might become recoupled.

The influence of romantic love has had many critics, particularly from the point of view of feminism. Many feminists have seen such notions of love as a snare for women, filling their heads with empty dreams and drawing them away from a more fulfilling autonomous life by creating emotional and economic dependence upon men. I don't believe this is accurate, as I tried to show in *The Transformation of Intimacy*. Ideals of romantic love were pioneered by women rather than men and to me are part of a drive to demand emotional communication and equality in relationships. In romantic love stories, emotional conquest prevails over sexual conquest: love is founded not on sexuality as such but upon admiration and respect for the qualities of the other. Romantic love is a dream and a projection and therefore lends itself to all sorts of cruelty and exploitation, as is also made plain in popular novels and romantic fiction. The ethos of seduction and abandonment, which is to some extent believed in by both sexes, not only men, jostles with ideals of intimacy and fidelity. These jostlings, however, are part of real life – they are in effect where we are at.

But couldn't 'falling in love' be seen as the very opposite of empowerment? The individual is impelled by a force he or she can't control. Our current ideas about love seem often to stress dependence rather than autonomy: 'I can't live without you', 'you are all the world to me', 'without you I'm nothing' and so forth. Popular songs are full of these sorts of sentiment.

Yes, to put things in current therapeutic jargon, autonomy vies with co-dependence in contemporary love relationships. So do stereotypical views of men and women – for instance, the male hero is aloof and ruthless (at least to start with) while the female (again to begin with) is submissive and perhaps treated cruelly. The underlying logic of tales of romantic love, though, is one of humanization and progressive equality. In popular culture, as studies have shown, most stories end happily, in a situation in which mutual respect and understanding are achieved, which then become the foundation of a renewed and deepened love. Of course, this is an idealization. Nevertheless we see refracted in these stories the confused but real trend of development that is occurring towards greater emotional democracy.

Just to press the objection a little further: couldn't romantic love be seen to stand in the way of forming a good and enduring relationship? Falling in love isn't particularly rational and it is not clear that it can be the basis for a long-term relationship, at least for most people. It could be seen as the sparking-point which brings people together, but in most marriages and relationships, heterosexual and non-heterosexual, this initial attraction comes to be overlain with everyday familiarity. Relationships which endure may then shift. They aren't any longer based upon romantic ideas but upon the working compromises that have to be made to live day in day out with another.

There is certainly some truth to that. I would be far from saying that romantic love, which in any case involves a complex of partly contradictory emotions and ideals, somehow fits functionally with the new world of constructed relationships. Romantic love, if I can put it this way, carried the promise of emotional equality, but was driven by the realities of its opposite, emotional inequality. It reflected the aspirations of women in a society becoming much more individualized, but still subject to the rule of patriarchy.

I don't know exactly how one would measure this, but I would guess that romantic love today is in a state of decline. Women have far greater real equality, economically and emotionally, than they had before and are less inclined to support a narrative based on different premises. Romantic love carried with it the idea of a lifetime steady-state commitment, but everyone becomes sceptical of this in a high-divorce high-remarriage society, which is what we have now. I would expect different ideals of love to be coming into being and one

can certainly see them in the self-help and therapeutic literature, which I regard as a kind of on-the-ground literature of
our reflexive engagement with our everyday lives. One of these
is what I call 'confluent love', love which is based on a learning process in a relationship, emotionally and sexually. This is
still a set of ideals, with only a loose relationship to reality, as
in the case of the romantic love complex.

*What of sexuality itself? What are the main changes happening
there?*

A basic aspect of patriarchal power was always emotional and
sexual. Until relatively recently, sexuality was dominated by
the division I referred to earlier between virtuous and non-
virtuous women, which was a vital underpinning of male
power. It was also central to all types of traditional family,
given the importance of tracing lines of inheritance and the
transmission of property. There are many examples of sexually liberated women to be found in history, but these are almost always either at the top or bottom of society – groups
who for contrasting reasons can break free from the dominant
norms. By and large women's sexuality was thoroughly confined, not only by conceptions of virtue and proper behaviour
but by the routines and problems of childbirth. Sexuality
and death for women were connected in quite a different
way from that suggested by de Rougement – rates of mortality
of women in childbirth in all traditional cultures were high
by current standards. The point is not so much that sexuality
was geared to reproduction as that reproduction enforced
certain sexual regimes. Sexuality has now become almost
entirely separated from reproduction, for both sexes – a change
of immense importance. The origins of this are not directly
bound up with improved techniques of contraception,

although these are to some degree the condition of such a transition. Rather, they come from the whole cluster of transformations involved with the dissolving economic basis of marriage and the demographic transition. Today, sexuality has become 'plastic' or detraditionalized. Plastic sexuality is sexuality which has to be invented and attached to its object: it is sexuality escaping from the schismatic image of women and from the imprint of heterosexuality too.

Recent years have seen the strong re-emergence of attempts to explain human behaviour, including sexuality, biologically or genetically. How would you reply to those who argue that sexuality is largely structured by genetic programming? It is argued, for instance, that there is an evolutionary explanation for male tendencies to promiscuity and for the more selective outlook of women. To what extent does the imprint of our evolutionary past impact upon changes affecting sexual behaviour today?

I'd like to distinguish several issues here. First, there has certainly been a change in the Zeitgeist since the time I started out in intellectual life. At that point cultural, rather than biological, theories of human activity were dominant and cultural relativism was common, although always controversial. Now all this has gone into reverse, not just because intellectual fashions change but no doubt in relation to the changed mood in the wider society. With the dissolution of Marxism and socialism, history no longer seems so malleable; and the rise of free-market philosophies has to some extent been reflected in the prominence which some Darwinian theories again enjoy today. The mood will at a certain point alter again and intellectual currents will change with it. I'm sure that at some point there will be a reaction against current forms of biological reductionism.

Second, we should separate Darwinianism or evolutionary psychology from the advances now being made in genetics. Whatever the wilder fancies which might be built around it, genetics is an area of science in the full flood of development. It is plainly having a revolutionary impact, particularly as connected with biotechnology. The Human Genome project surely isn't, as some of its advocates claim, going to provide a detailed blueprint of what we are as human beings – genetic inheritance always interacts with life experience and the environment. Yet the advances in genetics are demonstrable and concrete. I don't think the same could be said for evolutionary psychology, which is more speculative. It depends upon inferences upon a presumed evolutionary past and then applies these to interpret behaviour seen in the present. If men are more promiscuous than women, it is because there is an evolutionary advantage to men in spreading their attentions as far as possible, while the reverse is the case for women. But this is no more of an 'explanation' than functional 'explanations', which I referred to before, are. The only proper explanation would be one which did in fact reveal a genetic basis for male promiscuity, and no one is in a position at the moment to show that.

Human beings do have an evolutionary background and each individual has a genetic inheritance. It wouldn't make sense to suppose that these facts aren't relevant to how humans behave as well as to their physical makeup. But at the moment not much more than interesting speculations can be made. In any case, I fail to see their significance for contemporary debates about social and political reform. Let's suppose we could show that there is a genetically transmitted basis of differences in sexual behaviour between men and women. Little would flow from this as regards the consequences and implications of the changes affecting sexuality we see around us now. As cultural beings, we can overcome biological drives and demands, even very strong ones – human beings presumably have a strong drive to self-preservation, yet can commit suicide. The same is true from the other direction. Supposing we find that women become as promiscuous as men. In current sex surveys in the US and UK the proportion of married women who claim to have affairs is catching up rapidly with that of men. Does this mean that the evolutionary thesis is disproved? It doesn't, and for the same reason as before, that biological bases of behaviour can be over-ridden.

So far you seem to be talking almost exclusively about hetero-sexuality. How does the position of homosexuals and bisexuals fit with what you are saying?

The relation of homosexuality to the changes described above is complicated, but the cultural 'coming out' of homosexuals is deeply involved with the creation of plastic sexuality. The church in the West had an ambivalent and shifting attitude to homosexuality, as the historian John Boswell indicates. The sources for the past aren't complete, obviously, and Boswell's work itself has been criticized. What is clear is that homosexuality has been tolerated – quite often actively approved – in more cultures than it has been prohibited. We are talking here of male homosexuality, between individuals of certain ages or contexts. Homosexual activities, for example, are quite often tolerated between adolescent boys prior to marriage and between boys and older 'uncles' who are supposed to school them in the sexual arts. Valuation of love between young men as the highest ideal, as in classical Greece, seems rare historically and cross-culturally. The category of 'homosexual' nevertheless, as

Foucault says, seems to be a product of the past century. Few cultures appear to have a word for 'homosexual', except in the case of ritualized homosexuality and bisexuality, where the words to describe such individuals usually don't have a clear secular meaning.

I am interested in the evolution of homosexuality primarily in relation to wider trends affecting sexual behaviour in the late modern era. The end of nature and of tradition are the processes which have allowed for the flourishing of homosexuality, or gay culture if you like, in present-day society. I don't mean to underestimate the significance of the battles which have been fought for gay rights and against homophobic attitudes. But homosexuality could only disappear as a 'perversion' with the escape of sexuality from nature and the hold of tradition, including traditional forms of male sexuality. In the case of perversion, as so often elsewhere, nature and tradition were combined ideologically: homosexuality, along with a range of other sexual activities, was specifically 'unnatural'. An interesting reflexive twist is that, once these changes have happened, genetic interpretations of homosexuality can be taken over by a more confident gay culture as part of its very legitimacy.

I see gays as pioneers, particularly in the sphere of relationships. Gay culture, especially male gay culture, is often associated with an extreme version of that male promiscuity of which we have spoken. But the large majority of gay people of both sexes, like heterosexuals, at any one time are in coupled relationships. Until very recently – and even now only one or two countries are the exception – gay marriage has been an impossibility. Gays have therefore been forced to pioneer the more open and negotiated relationships which subsequently have permeated to the heterosexual population. Gays have been the emotional pioneers of modernity in respect both of sexuality and of intimacy, at least as I have defined them. Of course, homosexual couples often mimic – sometimes deliberately parody – the attitudes of the heterosexual community. Relations of power and submission similar to those of heterosexual marriage are constructed within homosexual relationships. There seems as much violence within gay relationships, involving both sexes, as within the heterosexual world. Yet as an uninstitutionalized form, standing apart from tradition, homosexual relationships did not incorporate institutionalized modes of power. Implicit equality, active trust and communication have been almost of necessity a basic part of gay relationships that endure over time. They also hit upon the problems, anxieties and insecurities inherent in detraditionalized relationships.

What of the theme of the body? You mention this a lot in your work on self-identity and in general it seems a theme which crops up in your later writings. How would you situate your own work as regards other authors who have made the body a prime focus – for example, Foucault's descriptions of the body and its pleasures, or Goffman's discussion of the body in his writings on total institutions and elsewhere?

I hope you'll forgive a somewhat philosophical digression at this point. In thinking about this issue I was influenced first of all – this is way back in the mid 1970s – by two somewhat disparate figures, both in philosophy – Merleau-Ponty and Wittgenstein. Merleau-Ponty was associated with phenomenology, but he distanced himself very effectively from the more cognitive emphases of his forerunners. He was very much concerned with themes of time and space and in his discussions of human action stressed the situated character of the agent. The agent is not an abstract 'subject' but is embodied, and the body is much more than just a physiological machine which accompanies the workings of consciousness.

For Merleau-Ponty, the flow of consciousness would be impossible without the continual monitoring of bodily response which both the agent and others with whom he or she is in interaction routinely carry on. Foucault in fact appears to have been influenced by Merleau-Ponty, even though he disregarded some of Merleau-Ponty's main ideas.

Wittgenstein strongly accentuated the contextual nature of language and consciousness. I interpreted the connection between the early and late Wittgenstein in the following way. In the *Tractatus* Wittgenstein famously concludes that there are limits to speaking about language in language. The later Wittgenstein suggests that the 'what can't be said in language' is what has to be done: the fixity and endless inventiveness of language both depend upon the involvement of language with everyday action and the competent actor. The meaning of words consists in how they are used within the flow of situated activity. Although he seems to have had few direct connections to the tradition, Wittgenstein seems to me more of a phenomenologist than a relativist. There is a reality, and common access to that reality is the condition of our mutual understanding. Our access to it is through our routine experiences, which both presume and are presumed by it. Thus to know the meaning of the word 'table' and what the differences are between a table and a 'chair' I must be familiar with what people do with chairs and tables, and this includes a taken-for-granted awareness of their sensory properties. Rather than speaking of consciousness and action as separate, Wittgenstein links them through the body, understood as the locus of agency. Body and self are much more integrated here than they are in the forms of philosophy, such as logical positivism, from which Wittgenstein sought to dissociate himself.

Goffman was not a philosopher. His ideas were rooted much more in G.H. Mead and symbolic interactionism, although Goffman did read Wittgenstein late on in his career. But to me there are close parallels between Wittgenstein and Goffman in spite of the very different style of their work – Wittgenstein was relentlessly serious, Goffman characteristically whimsical and playful.

It was Foucault who more than anyone else introduced the theme of 'the body' as such into contemporary social science. Paradoxically, Foucault was able to single out the body as a distinct focus of attention largely because he saw the body – or more accurately chose to see the body – as acted upon rather than acting. I don't think this was philosophical naïvety on Foucault's part as many have said. The last thing Foucault was was philosophically naïve. Foucault's concern with the 'docile body' was a strategic intellectual decision. He wanted to analyse the body reduced to passivity by the twin impact of moral servitude and organizational power. It is often said that Foucault's writings from *The History of Sexuality* onwards mark a break with his earlier conceptions both of the body and of power, but I would interpret this more as an attempt to shift conceptual gears. Foucault wasn't bothered about appearing inconsistent.

By using this strategy Foucault was certainly able to develop some counter-intuitive ideas. He was concerned to show that the Enlightenment ideology of expanding individual freedom created 'another side', the rigid constraints of disciplinary power. On the other hand, he was also able to show that the apparently morally rigid Victorian regime of sexuality was the ground for a flowering of sexual concerns.

I was never a direct follower of Foucault. I picked up some of Foucault's themes, such as the medicalizing of the body, but approached them quite differently. I used the other writers referred to in order to situate discussion of the body within a wider theory of action and the flow of consciousness – as well as in relation to reflexivity.

I have one last question in this area which follows on from all this. In the texts we've been talking about, you suggest, I think with some regret, that ethical and existential questions have been 'squeezed out' of modern political discussion. Do you think they are on their way back, and how would they be institutionally accommodated?

They are a part of what I call *life politics*. Life politics comes into being as a result of all these changes. There is a return of ethical debates to different spheres of life: from issues of body politics and genetics to a wide range of ecological themes. These issues are already pretty apparent: the family values debate is one example, the abortion debate is another.

Some questions of a moral or ethical kind have been raised because, as with genetic engineering for example, technology is making things possible that weren't possible previously . . .

Yes, but they are raised by the two processes I described earlier: the retreat of nature and the retreat of tradition. Tradition provided a framework for moral action as well as practical action, and nature, so to speak, took things out of play. Life politics is about how we live after the end of tradition and nature – more and more political decisions will belong to the sphere of life politics in the future.

Well, these sorts of issue have certainly risen in prominence, but there were earlier ethical questions. A generation ago, we were concerned with the ethics of inequality. Now this seems to have slipped down if not off the agenda. The question of the inequality of distribution is surely, in part, an ethical political question – yet it seems to have lost its contemporary resonance.

Inequality has certainly not gone off the political agenda, and nor have other issues of emancipatory politics. However, with respect to inequality – that is, economic inequality – liberalism has proved more enduring than socialism, certainly than the more radical forms of socialism. What has gone off the agenda is any kind of enforced egalitarianism. The costs have proved too great, and the drab uniformity which can result too oppressive. Partly as a response, political theory has turned towards equality of opportunity rather than of outcome – or, should I say, has returned to it. I don't believe such an approach is sufficient. Even if something close to a meritocratic society were attainable, it would have major problems and limitations. What would it be like, for example, to be at the bottom of the society and know that one deserved to be there? How could a society cope with the large amount of downward mobility there would be in a meritocratic society? And so forth. Egalitarianism may have gone, but equality of outcome has to stay on the agenda. In discussing inequality, however, one should remember that economic inequality is not the only type, and that in some respects – most notably in gender relations – inequality is decreasing rather than increasing.

Interview Six

Politics Beyond Left and Right

CHRISTOPHER PIERSON *I would like to talk about some more directly political issues. Political themes have often been implicit in your work, sometimes more explicit as in* The Nation State and Violence, *but it does seem that in the last three or four years you have had a heightened interest in political and indeed party political matters. Why has there been this shift in your attention towards political questions?*

ANTHONY GIDDENS I became more involved in day-to-day politics than I was before. I have spent more time thinking about the Labour Party and British politics than I did earlier. At the same time, like everyone else, I've been reflecting about what the future of politics might be in a world where socialism no longer appears as the avenue of the future.

Beyond Left and Right, *published in 1994, was widely discussed as a 'blueprint' of what a more radical politics could mean now, but I'd like to begin by asking why you think we are beyond left and right.*

The division between left and right hasn't disappeared – it is still meaningful, both in the context of party politics and in wider political thinking. Those on the left believe in promoting equality and hold this goal can be furthered by government action, whatever level of government is in question. The left believes that a market society has its limits and has a commitment towards the extension of democracy in various spheres of life, not just in the public sphere but in the other areas of contemporary democratization I have discussed. People on the right are more comfortable with inequality and are sceptical that government can or should seek to limit it. They may see inequalities as given by nature, or alternatively as properly enshrined in tradition.

There isn't much of a far left around any longer, but there is a far right. The far right now has a theory of globalization, and a reaction to it – essentially protectionism in the face of the global market, coupled to protectionism in respect of traditional forms of family, authority and the state. Although it has bizarre fringes, such as some of the militia groups in the US, such a view does have a certain consistency. It doesn't have the same paradoxical stance as neo-liberal conservatism, which favours open global markets on the one hand and traditional cultural values on the other. The far right is disturbing and dangerous because isolationism and protectionism, even when not coupled to xenophobia, lead to the same kinds of division that have endlessly produced wars and schisms in the past. With the decline of socialism and the contradictory nature of orthodox conservatism, left and right no longer offer a purchase on some of the most basic political issues we face. Ecological problems, for example, straddle the left–right division.

Let me put to you an 'old politics' objection to this view. Although you talk about socialism and capitalism elsewhere, you don't talk about them here (in defining left and right). You define socialism very strongly in terms of a system of economic management. You describe it as an appropriate form of economic organization for simple modernity but one that doesn't correspond to the kinds of way we live now. You suggest that socialism in this sense, if not all the ideas associated with it, is dead.

As a system of economic management, yes.

But there are two other senses in which people might see socialist ideas as still important: one is to say that socialism is concerned with unequal patterns of ownership, of property, and the other is to say that socialism is actually, at its simplest, the 'antidote' or the 'other' of capitalism. Critics might argue that you evade these two important aspects of socialism by making it solely an issue of economic planning.

They are the same, aren't they? Property always meant capital, surely.

We might gloss the first position by saying that socialism is concerned with the inequality of economic outcomes, which might not be exclusively because of differences in private property, but there is also the more generic sense in which socialism is the antidote to capitalism. In some sense, it could be said, you don't want to talk about socialism because you don't want to talk about capitalism.

Socialism is no longer an alternative to capitalism. I can't at the moment see any way around that. This is far from saying that the global market economy doesn't provoke all sorts of problem, for it does. But there isn't a coherent alternative society waiting around the corner any more. Unless you want to recommend market socialism as such a solution?

No. In Socialism After Communism, *I looked at market social-*
ism and concluded that it wasn't actually a very plausible model.
But not because it doesn't have ethically attractive features. And
do we need a fully fledged blueprint of an alternative social form
called socialism (or anything else) in order to be able to mount a
critique of capitalist institutions?

No, but critique is only effective if it leads to a better way of
doing things. There are many pointers. There's something in the
thesis put forward by Ingelhart about post-materialist values,
which only come into play beyond a certain level of economic
development – these concern what I would call life-political issues. There is something in the debate about global financial
markets – Soros and others are calling for greater regulation.* A
very important transition we are living through concerns the
possible disappearance of large-scale war. There is plainly something in the idea that the role and nature of the nation-state are
changing. All these offer possibilities as well as problems. To me
the goal is developing a cosmopolitan global society, based on
ecologically acceptable principles, in which wealth generation
and control of inequality are reconciled. I don't see this as wholly
utopian. I'm not sure it could be called socialism, even if the
ethical thrust of socialist thought is still there.

But surely you would not want to say that if there are capitalistic
inequalities in the world order we shouldn't say anything about
them simply because you don't think there are any ready solu-
tions? You were saying, I think, that critique is much easier but
less useful if it doesn't have some alternative agenda to put for-
ward, but if the alternative is simply to describe the world in

---

* George Soros: celebrated international financier and (latterly) social com-
mentator. See interview below, pp. 218–26.

ways which are amenable to change that's not necessarily such
an attractive alternative. I guess somebody who was being criti-
cal of what you are doing would say look, in talking about mo-
dernity you are stepping back to an earlier sociological medium
which didn't want to recognize the logic of capitalist forms of
economic organization.

I don't see that at all. Capitalism remains one of the great forces
shaping the world, although now more globalized and based
on an information economy.

Well, I don't want to offer some sort of monocausal alternative to
this. But I guess that somebody who was looking at what you
have said about these changes in late modernity and what you
say about the transformation of intimacy might well say that what
you do is radically de-emphasize in your account the most im-
portant aspect of change in the last twenty years, which is the
growth of global economic inequality. So it is not just the globali-
zation of economies, but it's a globalization of economies under a
particular capitalist logic which is not the same as it was in the
twenty-five years following World War II. So that, if you are re-
ally concerned about processes of democratization, the extension
of inequality and those kinds of thing you should actually focus
more attention on these economic processes.

I don't disagree with that. We must take a hard look at capitalism nowadays and what kinds of alternative or rough edge it
has. But I don't see a socialist alternative.

You have talked about four spheres of modernity, about the differ-
ent kinds of 'bad' associated with each of these spheres and about
the alternative to them. In talking about capitalism and problems
in the economic domain, you introduce the idea of a 'post-scarcity

society', again picking up the ecological theme. I wonder (1) what the post-scarcity economy is supposed to look like and (2) how and why would we get there.

Post-
scarcity

A post-scarcity economy is one where affluence produces problems which can't be dealt with by more affluence. It's not a society where there aren't any longer scarce goods. It doesn't refer to a society as a whole, but rather certain aspects of or areas within it.

Isn't the problem with global capitalism one about distribution, and some people not having enough, as much as it is about affluence?

Yes it is. But what isn't true is that most of the problems we confront can be traced to economic inequality or class.

Well, I'm just curious because you're talking about a post-scarcity society being on 'the other side of' capitalism . . .

Post-scarcity society connects closely with reflexive modernization – it is the society to which such modernization is appropriate. To repeat, we have too much of some things, at least in some sectors of society or parts of the world. This may now even include information: information may be becoming too abundant rather than too scarce, creating a problem of 'information smog'.

What I don't see in this is the prospective agency of change. There are some people who have a very strong vested interest in maintaining economic forms rather the way they are now, however much smog – informational or otherwise – that generates. Who are the agents of change in moving us towards a post-scarcity society?

In the world in which we now live, change is ever-present. Security and continuity are as important as generating further change. Beyond that the agents of change are the same as they long have been: states, groups of states, business firms, international organizations, plus the activities of ordinary people in their everyday lives. There are new strategies, of course, like bottom-up development, micro-credit and so forth, which are surely important and in line with real possibilities generated by the global system. Business corporations themselves are changing. Even in the largest – perhaps especially the largest – decentralizing and network structures have become the norm. The high-growth sectors are in smaller and medium companies rather than large companies. The big corporations aren't running rampant as many feared. We have to look where levers of policy are when we no longer have the historical magic of Marxism. It might all turn out badly, but that's what it's like to live in a risk society, where history offers no guarantees.

But there is a difference surely between having a teleological view that there are 'guarantees of history' and having a political agenda which identifies particular political actors with a potential for effective agency? You down-play the traditional politics of the left and the idea of historical agency founded in the working class in either a Marxist or even a reformist social democratic sense. You may well be right. But if that's all true, why should we think that we are likely to move from the kind of global market economy we have now towards a post-scarcity economy, when you have said that the people who have no interest in moving towards a post-scarcity society are in power?

For lots of reasons. The world is finite and sooner or later we run up against limits to growth, one of the defining features of a post-scarcity society. What we haven't got is a formula saying that this is how the world is going to be put to rights. Take global poverty. Consciousness of poverty isn't declining – those committed to contesting it include nation-states, non-governmental organizations, even business corporations. Some of this is posturing, but mostly the impetus is genuine enough. We can't be sure that the current emphasis on bottom-up development, community regeneration and so forth will work, but they are certainly worth trying. Asian capitalism may be in severe difficulties just now, but it has contributed to overcoming basic poverty in the countries involved. The 'rush to growth' of the Asian tiger economies has in fact brought them face to face with issues of post-scarcity – on the ecological front and in other areas too.

The threat of global catastrophe, on the other hand, is real. World financial markets could collapse. It could be that we have already done irreparable damage to the earth's ecosystems – no one knows. It's easy to be sanguine about all this; to say that there's too much scaremongering around and so forth. I already pointed to the dilemmas here before. We won't be rescued by 'history' but we can act in awareness of risk. Reflexive modernization is still a consciousness that most of the world is made now by human beings rather than being just given. We have to work with what there is.

I don't take a teleological view of change nor do I think that so-cialism is a kind of panacea which can simply be introduced and everything would be changed. What I was trying to address was a concern about where the fault lines and where the institutional problems actually lie in the existing global order. . .

The four-fold division of modernity is my way of saying where those problems lie: the growing divisions between rich and poor, plus the commodification of life (problems of the global capitalist economy); the suppression of human rights (problems of democracy); ecological issues (problems of the impact of science and technology); the minimizing of war (problems of military power).

I guess the issue here is whether you have actually given enough weight in those accounts to dysfunctions which are characteristic of capitalist forms of economic organization. A critic might say you're not allowing enough weight to the way in which the globalized capitalist economy generates a growth in global inequality of economic outcomes and that to focus on problems of affluence and post-scarcity is, in some sense, to draw attention away from these.

The picture is more complex than this. Developed capitalist economies surely have done better than any socialist economy. Free markets generate inequalities, but some types of capitalism can mute these; and there are normally other factors involved. The difficulties of Africa, for example, clearly reflect its particular colonial past. Only if one has a very deterministic view of capitalism could one simply say 'capitalism is the culprit'.

I'm not entirely persuaded that the fact that the Soviet economy wasn't very good or that there aren't any very attractive existing models of post-capitalist forms of economic organization means that one should downgrade the extent to which one explains whatever problem it is on the basis of economic organization. You can't say that capitalism isn't important because we don't have an alternative system that's any more attractive.

But what alternatives do you suggest, unless you are still saying that socialism is somehow still alive or that it could be revived on a global level? If you are saying that free-market capitalism produces inequalities, and that these inequalities are getting worse, that's possibly true. But it doesn't provide any counter-mechanisms.

I was always against the idea of trying to make the notion of capitalism do too much explanatory work – as it often did in the past for those on the left and now, I suppose, for some of its more freewheeling advocates on the right.

I certainly don't want to defend some sort of primitive claim that 'Socialism is the answer'. There's not much value in talking about some kind of undifferentiated capitalism, without the kinds of distinction into different regime types and different species which the better analyses now make. The argument I was trying to press is that I thought you have chosen to talk about modernity, rather than to talk about capitalism, in part because there were prospective solutions in terms of changing modernity which didn't present themselves, as you suggest, in terms of changing economic forms of organization. You seem to suggest that this form of economic organization is basically all that there is: global markets based on existing kinds of property relationship.

Modernity does have these institutional complexities I've talked about. Whatever is happening to it now, the nation-state, for instance, is bound up with the wider changes of the modern era, as agent and as acted-upon. I don't see how it could be seen as an artefact of capitalism. Nation-states have helped shape the capitalist economy. Consider, for example, the current era of global markets. Governments have contributed to this in an active and conscious way by liberalizing, by privatizing. One of the main components of global financial markets is government bonds. Governments are borrowing from a private global pool of capital part of what they previously got from taxation within the nation-state. That produces a perverse situation when those markets then become controlling influences over them. A good deal of the content of financial markets consists of the buying and selling of government bonds against other assets. Government bonds are just a way of getting loans from international capital. This process is driven by a sort of mixture of ideologies, forms, institutions.

Well, of course, I wouldn't want to present any argument in a crude sense! And I wouldn't argue that states are not involved in this – or any other – phase of capitalist development. Any adequate description of capitalism could not be exclusively confined to private economic actors. States have always been a part of capitalism whatever generically that is supposed to mean. They have been involved in making markets and creating markets. They have been involved in managing relations between capital and labour. All of these kinds of thing have always been done by states. So I don't think there is any capitalism without the state.

Why not then recognize states and capitalist markets as two partly independent influences upon the global order? The nation-state system interacts with the capitalist economy, but the one can't be reduced to the other. Why not accept that? It is consistent with recognizing the dynamic role of capitalism.

I wouldn't want to sublimate everything under the mono-logic of a driving world capitalism. But, whilst I certainly don't accept the view that globalization has rendered states powerless, I do believe that the governing capacity of states has been altered by the kinds of change you refer to as globalization. Certain things that governments might wish to do are just much more difficult now.

But if you're not saying that capitalism is the driving force in all these changes, then there must be other forces, not driven by the same dynamics, in play. Market forces don't operate autonomously. Governments decided to liberalize and privatize in response to the failure of socialism and the end of Keynesianism. As they liberalize, they create the very sorts of market form that they find it hard to control. It doesn't follow that those market forms have some sort of causal primacy. So one is always driven back to a multi-dimensional notion of modernity. The reorganization of military power and the actions of rogue states, including the adventures of Saddam Hussein, aren't simply produced by capitalism. Military power is military power and has its own impact.

The same thing is true of our interaction with nature through science and technology. There is now a world community of scientists busy making discoveries and constructing theories. These processes are only partly driven by market imperatives. They are fuelled by a quest for scientific standing and prestige in a global community geared to the production of knowledge.

Perhaps we could move on to consider your views about the welfare state. How would you characterize the welfare state and its current difficulties?

The welfare state can be seen as a risk management system, not just a way of redistributing between rich and poor – or as a way of controlling the poor, which is after all where its early origins lie. It is essentially a social or collective insurance system. Questions about the welfare state are not just who pays, who gains and who loses, but how we should balance security and risk – in a world where the nature of risk is changing.

*I wonder about some issues of periodization and causation here.
You might argue that one of the causes of the heightened percep-
tion of risk now is to do with the threatened removal of some the
apparatuses of social insurance which people have previously re-
lied on. But these forms of security are really of very recent origin
– certainly much newer than modernity. As you describe it, the
era of welfare state social insurance lasts less than fifty years.
And surely if you want to explain why things are changing in this
area you have to look to a whole series of other changes – changing political forces and capacities of the state – rather than the
changing context of risk.*

The welfare state is as such relatively recent, although surely
not confined to the post-war period. But welfare states and
other social insurance systems were never as capable, universal or protective as one might imagine. It's not as if we are
progressing from a world of total security to one of insecurity. The welfare state was always a way of handling contingency and protecting individuals against risk and was
therefore closely associated with the insurance principle.
Welfare states, however, were built on the presumption of
what I earlier called external risk. The state will step in to
protect you if things go wrong – citizens aren't assumed to
be too involved with things going wrong. Now we have shifted
to a much more active, reflexive risk environment in which
people have a different relationship to their futures, their
bodies, their social and economic involvements. I don't think
this means junking the welfare state, but it does point to
radical reform. Many look back to a golden age of the welfare system, but it was a much more mixed experience than
they would have us believe. There is a left nostalgia for the
welfare state, based partly on fiction. Anyone who has stood
in line to collect unemployment benefits, or struggled against

welfare bureaucracies, must recognize that the welfare state has long had its negative side. Welfare dependency, the suboptimal outcomes of welfare systems – these are real. I'm not in favour of the neo-liberal onslaught on welfare. We need a positive restructuring of welfare institutions, which will allow people to take more active attitudes to risk but at the same time will give them protection. That means exploring forms of insurance mechanism which are not so closely related to welfare receipts. As far as possible, rather than giving people goods we should give them capabilities and responsibilities.

The welfare state was never a pure insurance mechanism. States were always trying to achieve or deliver some other goals at the same time.

. . . like exercising social control of the population, keeping people in their place . . .

But they were also trying to guarantee some kind of minimum level of provision which it was then presumed private insurance markets wouldn't generate. As you've said earlier, we surely need a multi-dimensional account of the rise of welfare states. In part, policing and resisting social disruption, certainly, but also, in part, a response to pressure for a minimum base which reflected the capacities of various groups in society to mobilize behind this cause. You don't subscribe to the view of the welfare state as simply an agency of social control, do you?

No, that was simply an element of it.

I also wonder to what extent you are tempted to overstate the element of personal responsibility.

It's not just personal responsibility. It's also about how we apply insurance principles in relation to risk-taking and what role government should have in that. We should try to think imaginatively about these questions. It would, in principle, be possible for the government to issue redeemable bonds for social risk, not that any government has tried it. But there are already derivatives which cover disaster risks, for example. Liability is also an intriguing notion. What aspects of things that can go wrong should be covered, by whom, and for what aspects should one be responsible oneself?

But aren't the consequences of those kinds of change, to raise another rather 'old-fashioned' point, likely to be that the people who are well organized, affluent and well informed, and who are generally less costly to insure and better able to insure themselves, will end up with a better deal than those people who were not so well placed initially?

. . . a kind of double stratification . . .

So, in fact, you get a greater diversification through going the private route.

The division isn't just between public and private, but in how risks are faced and responsibilities cultivated. This is part of the reason why education seems to be opening up a bigger economic fault line than before. The educated person is better able to survive and prosper in an active, reflexive world.

Didn't Sweden, to some extent, achieve some level of social equalization through welfare state institutions?

Scandinavian welfare states show a lower degree of inequality than most other Western countries. But there is a real question as to whether this is a result of the welfare state or whether the welfare state reflects other aspects of Scandinavian society. There does seem to be a long-standing culture of equality and collective responsibility, for whatever reason.

Well, that may be true, but it certainly makes a good prima facie case for saying that actually welfare state institutions can be a way of embedding equalization, even if you want to say the source is that the Swedes want to be equal, in a way that Italians don't.

Yes, although this has been achieved in Scandinavia more through the redistribution of work than of income. The welfare state provides work for people (women, mostly) who in other societies are pushed into marginal jobs or out of the labour market altogether.

But it had to do with corporatism as well . . .

I don't think there is evidence that the welfare state in Sweden produced a direct redistribution of income or wealth, because on the level of wealth Sweden is actually quite unequal, a capitalistic society with a lot of wealthy families in it.

Someone like Esping-Andersen may well argue that a welfare state of that character actually addresses the point in terms of primary distribution and not in redistribution. That is, a whole set of institutional structures means that society gives everyone that wants it work, at a reasonable kind of wage, with the central negotiation of wages and conditions. So you don't need the welfare state apparatus to do all that kind of work.

Well, you do, because without a large welfare state there wouldn't be the jobs.

But that has a very important gender element as well, obviously . . .

Yes, but again in the Scandinavian countries there seems to be a moral culture of equality between the sexes, not wholly created by the welfare state. The vast majority of non-married and lone mothers in Scandinavian countries work in jobs in the welfare state. That does therefore look more like the redistribution of work than of income.

Except that there has also always been a huge budget for retraining and not very much expenditure on unemployment. But under these circumstances, benefit levels were still high and maternity rights much more extensive than they are in the UK.

But it's hard to see it as a model for the future. The only Scandinavian society that seems to have sustained it without other specific external resources, like Norway's, is Denmark. The Swedish system seems to be under severe strain. Finland has high rates of unemployment. Denmark and Holland seem to be the two successful intact welfare states with a good competitive position in the external economy. They are both small countries, which might have something to do with it.

A couple of final questions. In discussing the possibilities for positive welfare, you raise the idea of social 'pacts' between rich and poor. How do you imagine these might be established and operate?

For example, the refurbishment of London Underground might get widespread support from people in different tax brackets.

Once traffic and pollution have got bad enough, all London-
ers are 'in it together'. New alliances concerning other issues
could grow up between younger and older people – many in
both categories do depend on the state. To take another illus-
tration, think what the single currency might do. It might create alliance groups across Europe that no one has yet
anticipated, maybe a Europe-wide association of pensioners.

*I am not sure about this. It sounds as if what you are really talk-
ing about are public goods of some kind. Everyone stands to gain
from having a better Underground system, the rich and the poor
alike, even if it is only so that the streets aren't clogged up with
people when you drive down them in your posh motor. In this
instance, the rich have a direct gain. It's not clear, though, why
they should really want to do something redistributive. This has
always been a part of the rationale for redistribution through
welfare states anyway: the rich would give a little bit away, the
better to secure the bulk of what they had.*

Why do you find it problematic, then? It's a way of looking
for new solutions to such issues.

*And finally . . . You carry the tag of being Tony Blair's favourite
social scientist and your ideas, about positive welfare and reflexive modernization, for example, have been seen to have some sort
of 'elective affinity' with certain ideas of New Labour. I want to
ask what you make of the New Labour 'project'.*

One could see New Labour as a party which has simply shifted
to the right, and has cynically taken on board large chunks of
a Thatcherite programme. I don't believe such is the case. I
would like to think New Labour is pioneering an agenda that
relates to all the changes we've been talking about. One

shouldn't see this in too parochial a way – all ex-socialist parties, and parties of other political complexions too for that matter, are wrestling with these problems. So the political consequences of the developments we've mused over in this book certainly do not stand or fall by whatever happens to any one particular party in one specific country.

Interview Seven

World Politics

CHRISTOPHER PIERSON   *We spoke about politics earlier, but in the next sections I'd like to probe a little more deeply and also ask you to relate your ideas to events and changes in the international arena. Could I start by asking what you think the role of government is today? Many people speak of the end of politics and the end of government.*

ANTHONY GIDDENS   Can I begin by saying a little about the theme of endings in general? Literary critic Frank Kermode wrote his book *The Sense of an Ending* over thirty years ago now, but the theme of endings has become even more marked now than it was then. The end of socialism, Marxism, history, work, the family, the nation-state and even science – all of these, and others besides, have been the titles of recent books. What does this absorption with endings mean? Will intellectuals at some point declare an end to endings and start again to talk about beginnings?

The easy answer would be to say that all this comes from living near the closing of the millennium. Perhaps when the new century gets under way, a change in cultural sensibility will happen and we'll all start speaking of beginnings rather than endings. This hypothesis at least has the virtue of being testable, although we'll have to wait some years yet. I've contributed my little bit to all the talk of endings by introducing concepts such as 'post-traditional society', the end of nature and tradition and so forth.

However, I believe we should wrench ourselves away from the mind-set of endings. There is in fact a beginning occurring – the formation of a global cosmopolitan society in the sense which we've discussed in previous chapters. This is not a new era emerging from the old in the way Marx thought. Modernity is still modernity, but now much more universalized and radicalized via the global information revolution and other changes. Talk of endings for me represents an inability to come to terms with the limitations, complexities and paradoxes of modernity. We have to release ourselves from some of the dreams of the past, without abandoning the idea that we should seek to shape our own history. In a certain sense we have no choice but to continue the attempt to influence history, because our lives are shaped so fundamentally by the historical forces we have released. Consider, for example, our view of the future. Only the most naïve of techno-enthusiasts could any longer see the future as an open and available territory. One could almost say that for us the future has ceased to exist. Our very preoccupation with it creates a diversity of future scenarios – all thinking about the future for us has become scenario thinking, where any and every scenario can in principle influence the state of affairs it envisages. This isn't just an example of saying we can't know the future, which of course is logically true. Our way of thinking of what the future is has altered. This is true both of more collective issues and of our individual lives.

I haven't forgotten that the question you asked was about politics and government! But ideas of 'progressive' government were strongly linked to the idea of becoming the masters of our own history. It is a notion which goes well beyond socialism – and one that conservatism always resisted. Conservatives stressed the imperfectibility of human beings, the fragmentary nature of knowledge and our limited capacity to control the future. It might be said that we are all conservatives now – we need as often to put a brake upon change as further it; and we have to have a defensive or precautionary attitude to forces which we cannot hope fully to control. Our ideas about government and politics should reflect these new understandings.

Those who speak of the end of government and the end of politics are normally not only speaking of factual trends, but are advocating a particular value-position. The neo-liberals, for instance, want to shrink government down to its smallest essentials. Let markets take care of everything and let most of what we call 'political' sink back into civil society. They suppose that if a civil society is left to its own devices it will somehow automatically engender mechanisms of solidarity. Burke's 'little platoons' are often dragooned into service here, as if everything could be reduced to the small-scale. Such writers, in a grotesque way, blame the welfare state for sucking civil society dry and destroying 'natural' social harmony. This is the other side of the fence to the exaggerated claims made for the welfare state by some social democrats.

In a globalizing society, it is ridiculous to suppose that everything can be reduced down to the local level. Social solidarity depends upon good government at all levels, going right the way through from the local to emerging systems of global governance. There won't be an end to politics, but we do need to pioneer forms of government different from those of the classical nation-state. Special-interest groups and non-governmental organizations, now proliferating on the global scene, can't themselves provide mechanisms of government, because part of the very point of government is to resolve the different claims made by special-interest groups. There are real possibilities in David Held's model of 'cosmopolitan democracy', where he envisages forms of democratic association going right the way through from local government to reformed global institutions.

Surely, though, there is not an emerging world government? At the end of the last century, the idea that some form of world government was about to come into being became very popular and at least some people were convinced by it. World War I destroyed all that and such aspirations now look quite unrealistic. You yourself talk about a 'runaway world'. Doesn't this mean that we are now caught up in a set of forces – particularly those involved with global finance markets – to which we have to adapt, but which we have rather little hope of controlling?

I do think we live in a runaway world, an expression I originally borrowed from the anthropologist Edmond Leach. It was the title of his Reith Lectures some quarter of a century ago. He put a question mark after the phrase, though. In the light of developments since then I don't believe we need the question mark any longer. Yet we shouldn't, and can't, give up hope. We can't tame history in the manner Marx thought, because there aren't the dialectics of historical change upon which he based his theory. But as individuals, and as collective humanity, we can still hope to have greater control over our fate than is the case at the moment – indeed the future of world society depends on this. The cultural sensibility of the past thirty years, including the profusion of endings, has been considerably influenced by the impact of market fundamentalism, as contained within neo-liberal theory. If deregulation is all, then of course we cede control to them. This is the situation, coupled as it is to the globalizing of scientific innovation, which has created the runaway world.

There is an abstract side to this and a more concrete one. On a philosophical level, while recognizing the limitations of Enlightenment, we shouldn't relinquish the goal of giving some directive form to our history. The complicated reflexivity of this situation cuts both ways: predictions made which become self-fulfilling prophesies, for example, can go awry, but also can give us real purchase on future change.

On a somewhat more concrete level, there are many possibilities for upgrading and democratizing global governance which fall far short of world government. We have to include the role of global finance markets within such considerations. Market fundamentalists, of course, presume that financial markets are self-regulating and always tend, even in the short run, to equilibrium. Keynes was much more realistic, as is George Soros. As I do, Soros makes use of the notion of reflexivity. He argues that, because of the reflexive appropriation of information, financial markets tend towards instability – markets can move in unexpected ways, become chaotic, can be influenced by bandwagon effect, herd behaviour and panics. I agree with this view – global finance markets belong in the category of high-consequence risks which we have created for ourselves. Instantaneous real-time markets of the sort that we find today did not exist before and we can't even rule out the possibility that there could be a wholescale economic collapse.

We have to hope that large-scale meltdown is extremely unlikely. Yet we must surely look for ways to shape the flow of financial markets more effectively, so that processes of capital flight and panic are minimized. There has been a great deal of discussion of these issues in the world community following the problems experienced in the East Asian economies in 1997 and after. There was the same excitement after the Mexican devaluation crisis, but this later faded away and nothing came of it. I hope more will emerge this time. We have to look for a system which has more stability, which protects local economies – especially emerging market economies – from extreme market volatility. There are enormous pools of mobile capital in the world now, much of such capital looking for high short-term returns and concerned with profiting from changes in exchange rates. Large amounts of capital can be attracted to a particular country or region then suddenly, almost overnight, flood away from them. The smaller, open economies seem most vulnerable, but since this is a systemic problem even large developed economies could be badly affected.

Introducing more conscious governance into the system should be a prime goal. This could be achieved by a combination of local and global measures. The widespread introduction of local 'best practices' is important. One much-quoted example is the reserve system in Chile. Money can be invested in the country only if a deposit at zero interest is made with the central bank for a year. The object is to discourage short-term financial speculation without inhibiting investment, and this seems to have worked.

Changes in the International Monetary Fund seem both desirable and necessary, always supposing that institution is maintained in its current form. Less dominance by the US, greater transparency and other changes could fairly easily be achieved. Market regulation could be linked to democratization in a more effective way than has been achieved hitherto. Soros's suggestion of an international credit insurance corporation hasn't been taken very seriously, but something like this is worth considering. The idea would be to guarantee international loans up to a credit ceiling, linked to an assess-

Gov't bonds?

ment of the credit position of a particular country; beyond this level, private financial institutions wishing to lend would be on their own. In my view in addition a Tobin tax (placing a levy on international financial transactions) should be on the agenda. It isn't as unrealistic a possibility as is often suggested. It would have the double effect of discouraging wilder financial speculation and generating income which could be reappropriated by governments. After all, a good many of the transactions in world financial markets are to do with government bonds. Governments issued these bonds as a response to the reluctance of their citizens to pay high enough taxes to support well-developed welfare institutions. It wouldn't be easy to establish such a system, but its advantages would be considerable.

Tobin tax

Could the European Union be an effective means of protecting its members against shocks from financial markets? Do you see the other trading blocs which are emerging as offering a counterbalance to the chaotic tendencies of finance markets?

There is no way the European Union could stand alone on this issue, much less the other trading blocs, which are less well organized. Measures have to be taken on a more global level, without compromising the very real economic benefits which globalized capital markets can confer upon both developed and emerging economies. The fate of the Euro won't be settled by Europe but precisely by the reactions of global markets.

What is your own attitude to the single currency? Is there a sociological as opposed to an economic angle on it?

As an abstract concept, I'm not in favour of the single currency in the way in which it has been developed by the European Union. Other things should have come first. Problems of democracy and accountability in the EU are still acute and wait to be tackled. Declining public enthusiasm for the European Union is surely connected to the remote and bureaucratic nature of its institutions, plus the fact that its agenda doesn't seem to correspond to the issues which most worry ordinary people, notably unemployment. In addition, however, the single currency is a big risk, with unknown consequences – it fits closely with the open-ended nature of new risk phenomena. No group of states as large or wealthy as the EU has tried to institute a single currency before. In the past the formation of currencies has normally followed the creation of nation-states.

There is already considerable convergence among some of the European economies, so in the short term there might not be much market reaction to the Euro, although again no one really can be sure. The medium term could produce greater difficulties, depending upon the state of the world economy and the subsequent internal development of the various economies of Europe. Many say that the single currency is more of a political than a sheerly economic project, and I think this is right. However, anything which goes wrong with it economically will have major political consequences. The fears which many economists have expressed about the rigidities the single currency might impose are to my mind real. Europe doesn't have, and probably wouldn't want, the levels of labour mobility found in the US.

As you imply, sociologists should take a closer look at monetary union than they have so far. If its economic consequences are indeed radical – as both supporters and opponents in their different ways claim – then the social implications could be profound too. For example, as mentioned before, the single currency might result in groups from different countries seeing their common interests more clearly than before. A small farmer in southern Italy might discover that he shares a good deal in common with a Scottish crofter. Pensioners in one country might link together in an active way with their counterparts across Europe. The Euro might rebound on the political legitimacy of the EU rather than push it forward.

There is yet another possibility. It's a bit unlikely, but it might be that the Euro is a damp squib. The fact that economic convergence already exists may mean that not all that much will change.

What is your view of the EU as a whole? What is its likely future? Some see a growing tide of Euro-scepticism across the EU. Does this mean that, in spite of the Euro, the 'European project' is slipping backwards?

The European Union, like so much else in the world, has to be seen now as both an expression of and a response to globalization. The EU was born in quite a different context from that of today. It was initially a reaction to the destructiveness of World War II and later a Cold War phenomenon, situating 'Europe' between Communism on the one side and the United States on the other. Even some of the earliest advocates of European unity saw it in terms of the containment of Russia, with Europe as a 'free zone' between the Communists and the United States.

Things look very different post-1989 and it isn't surprising that the European project is carried along by a sort of inertia from the past. I am very pro-European, but we shouldn't ignore the criticisms made by some of the Euro-sceptics. Europe will become 'real' to the general population, to repeat, only if the EU helps address people's everyday concerns and does so within a framework of democratized institutions. In

particular, the principle of subsidiarity must be taken seriously. The term itself is a bit 'Euro bureau', a product of the
Brussels bureaucracy. However, it is basic to tracking globalization politically. 'Europe of the regions' shouldn't just be a
slogan, but a reality of the decentralization of power. To see
this is to recognize the fallacy of the idea that the European
Union, if it is to be anything, has to be a centralized federal
state. This is part of the Euro-sceptic nightmare, but properly
understood and developed the idea of Europe pushes in two
directions. Critics of federalism don't seem to realize that an
effective federal system is a decentralized one. Such a system
is compatible with developing the powers of European central government, so long as that goes along with an expansion
of democracy. The further development of bureaucracy at the
European level means strengthening the power of the European Parliament, but also looking afresh at forms of local accountability.

In spite of its inertial nature, the European Union is ahead
rather than behind the other economic blocs. The European
Union is, or can be reinterpreted as, a pioneering response to
the global order. It could develop as a model for other regions
to follow, and could contribute to the cosmopolitan global
society of which I spoke earlier.

The cosmopolitan character of Europe seems to me more
important than discovering some form of overall cultural identity for it. A great deal of effort has been expended to find
distinctive qualities of European culture which mark it off
from other civilizations, or to cultivate some sort of integrated
culture. But I don't think these strategies are either desirable
or necessary. Europe won't and can't look like a super nation-
state, with a common culture. The ideals which bind it together should be ones that anyone in the world can share,
including the promotion of economic prosperity, the protec-

tion of individual freedoms, collective responsibility towards the underprivileged and the recognition of democratic rights.

Parallel comments could be made about NATO, which everybody treats as a problem, but which could be a solution to some of our global dilemmas. The Americans have a central place in NATO and this marks it off from the European Union as such. As it stands NATO couldn't be the military arm of the EU. But this isn't a bad thing if we see NATO not for what it was – the quintessential Cold War organization – but as what it could become. It is often said that NATO has no clear role; but people who comment in this way still tend to be thinking of the armed forces in relation to traditional geopolitics and the clash of nation-states. NATO more properly belongs to a world where 'no one has any enemies' – that is, where geopolitics driven by the principles of Clausewitz's classic text *On War* no longer apply. NATO's presence declares the obsolescence of traditional war and its very amorphous structure could contribute to that situation. Seen in this way, there is no difficulty about the eventual expansion of NATO eastwards to include not only Eastern Europe, where it has got to at the moment, but also Russia.

The goals of NATO would have to be clarified in relation to such a scenario and its powers both more clearly defined and circumscribed. This could best be done by collaboration between the US and Europe working in conjunction with the United Nations. I would see such possibilities as falling squarely within the purview of utopian realism; these are aspirations which aren't easy to achieve but which are by no means unrealistic.

What of the economic condition of the EU, though? It is here that the term 'Eurosclerosis' is most often applied. As we speak, the American economy seems in good shape. There might or might not be a 'new paradigm' with a flattened business cycle, as some

*say; but the US have what appears to be a mix of low unemploy-
ment, low inflation and reasonable growth rates. Europe on the
other hand seems mired in high unemployment with little prospect of substantial reduction in the future. Many state-owned industries in leading European countries seem uncompetitive. Does
the 'European model' needs to be radically rethought?*

I would resist any such facile comparisons. The economist
Stephen Nickell has shown that there are large variations in
unemployment rates across Europe. Over the period 1983 to
1996, 30 per cent of the population of OECD Europe lived in
countries with average unemployment rates lower than those
of the US. Moreover, those with some of the lowest rates of
unemployment, such as Austria, Portugal or Norway, aren't
noted for the flexibility of their labour markets. If one looks
at growth rates, at least as these are ordinarily measured, some
European countries have had higher growth rates over this
period than the US. So the picture isn't quite as clear cut as
many assume. In addition, when comparing Europe and the
US there are all the points normally made by defenders of the
European welfare states. The US might have lower rates of
unemployment than most Western European countries, but
at the cost of having a higher proportion of working poor.
Wages of the bottom 25 per cent in the US have been stagnant
for a quarter of a century, or were so until very recently. This
hasn't been true of the leading Western European economies.
The prison population per head is very much higher than in
Europe. The most exhaustive study I've seen of this suggests
that imprisonment accounts for a full 2 per cent of the male
US labour force, if one includes not just men in prison but
those working in the prison service – the male unemployment rate would otherwise be 2 per cent higher.

We have to find a different way, and it is by no means an

impossible task. We talked about reform of the welfare state earlier, at least in a general fashion. Welfare reform is urgent and necessary in many European countries, although we should certainly recognize the diversity of European welfare states. Such reform should not be 'American': in other words, it should have a positive rather. than negative approach to welfare. 'Welfare' in the US has always had a negative tone. In Europe, on the other hand, the welfare state has quite rightly been seen as a springboard to social mobility and individual achievement. We need to press those qualities further in circumstances that have changed greatly since welfare systems were first set up, to achieve that new balance of risk and security which I referred to in an earlier chapter.

Welfare reform these days must be geared to economic success in the global economy. On the vexed question of labour markets, Stephen Nickell's analysis provides part of the answer. Labour market rigidity doesn't harm employment if this means the legal protection of workers' rights and strict employment legislation. Unemployment is linked to other characteristics, such as high unemployment benefits that run on indefinitely, or poor educational standards at the lower end of the labour market. Here structural changes definitely need to be made. In spite of the 'lump of labour' argument, I think there are important possibilities around the active redistribution of work. The success of the 'Dutch model', for instance, seems to depend upon the organized creation of a good deal of part-time work.

The issue of unemployment can't be looked at independently of the questions of gender and the family, or the more enveloping problem of the future of work as a whole. Rates of unemployment look like hard statistics but even under cursory examination turn out to be complex and interpretative. The unemployed are those who say they want to work. Even if this could be measured with precision, it leaves aside those who are working but would prefer not to be, who are working in unrewarding jobs – or who are left out of the category of the unemployed, such as those who are retired. Many people over the official retirement age might want to work, but they don't count as unemployed.

Contrary to those in the 1960s who predicted the emergence of a leisure society, work has increased its importance in people's lives rather than the reverse, if only because of the much higher proportion of women now in the labour force. Yet work remains oppressive for many people and today this includes even some working in managerial and professional occupations. There are two forms of oppression by time in the contemporary global economy. Those at the top tend to be always working: the old idea of the 'leisure class' has more or less completely disappeared. The impact of information technology and new communications technologies means there is no time when they are not working. They are oppressed by 'never having any time'. At the bottom of the society are those who suffer from another form of oppression – the unemployed have 'too much time' on their hands. One group could do with working less, the other with working more.

Unfortunately, redistribution of work from top to bottom isn't possible. The work situation of those in both categories, however, could be improved by more flexibility. 'Flexibility' can be a name for the casualizing of labour. Applied in a positive way, however, it can be the means of finding a more satisfying role for work in life. Those who have managed actively to reorder their lives in this way do claim to be happier for it. In German studies, these individuals have been called 'time pioneers' – they look to establish a different model of a work career from those that have predominated before.

A debate about the future of work was initiated by the German Greens in the early 1980s. Some ideas they produced were discounted as bizarre, but have since become part of mainstream discussion, even if not implemented – such as the notion of a citizen's income. Originally, ecological thinking seemed incompatible with economic development and job creation, but it has now become almost conventional to see the two as going hand in hand. More can be produced from less, and information technology is clean in an environmental sense whatever the other problems and difficulties it might create.

We don't know how far the further advance of information technology will destroy more jobs than it creates. Some, like Jeremy Rifkin, see the new technologies as moving up the job hierarchy in a destructive way. Having eliminated a good deal of unskilled and semi-skilled work, IT will next remove many of the jobs done by more qualified individuals. Others, including most orthodox economists, assume that the progress of the new technologies will create as yet unanticipated forms of demand, thereby generating as many jobs as are dissolved by technological development. The gap between these predictions only serves to re-emphasize the importance of not confining debates about work to the issue of unemployment alone.

So far we haven't talked about Britain's involvement in the EU. All the way through from the evolution of the European Steel and Coal Community to the European Union, Britain seems to have been on the sidelines. For all the talk of Britain becoming at the heart of Europe, nothing much seems to have changed. As an island, the UK has always had a separate history from the Continent; as an empire, it was linked historically with parts of the world other than Europe; and as an English-speaking country, it enjoys a close affiliation with the US. Taking all these together, what are the prospects for Britain's fuller integration within Europe?

Economically, the UK is already part of Europe: 60 per cent of the trade of the country is with the European Union. Paris is closer by plane or by train to London than is Manchester. I think the old attitudes are likely to change pretty rapidly now. No doubt the country will retain its transatlantic ties, but rather than being an outpost of the US on the edge of Europe, it could and should play a role in developing a continuing dialogue between Europe and the US.

Involvement in the EU is helping to reshape what Britain is as a nation. Those who are hostile to the European Union, of course, see this as draining away the sovereignty of the country and diluting its identity. On the whole, the contrary is true. Globalization tends to accentuate demands for local autonomy, including local nationalism. The best way to contain these, and to make regionalism and national identity compatible, is through the EU. Spain, with its autonomous regions, has provided a model for this and Britain is likely to follow something of a similar path. National identity can be preserved through decentralization rather than necessarily undermined by it.

So far we have been talking mainly about the developed world. One of the criticisms often made of your work is that you focus only upon this rather small segment of world society, ignoring the rest – the South. How would you respond to such a criticism?

That criticism made some sense when the globe was fairly clearly divided into First, Second and Third Worlds. Now we are in a situation where those divisions no longer apply. Some

erstwhile Third World countries are now richer than others
in the First World, while the Communist societies of Russia
and Eastern Europe no longer exist. In these circumstances,
most of my arguments apply more or less the world over. Globalization, as I have stressed earlier, is no longer primarily a
matter of the expansion of the West across the rest of the world.
'Third World' characteristics are to be found in the very midst
of the affluent countries. So I don't think I could be said to
ignore the major part of the world, although it is true that I
haven't made any detailed studies of societies in the South.

*Perhaps I could ask you for your reflections continent by conti-
nent, North and South. First, what do you see as the main problems facing the 'transitional economies' of Eastern Europe and
Russia?*

Russia is in a different situation from any of the East European countries. In Eastern Europe, one of the factors influencing a successful transition to a market economy and a liberal
democracy is how far ruling party elites were displaced early
on. Countries like Slovakia or Romania aren't in good shape
while others, like the Czech Republic, Hungary and Poland,
are even close to being accepted within the European Union.
The past history of a country, including whether or not it previously had established parliamentary institutions, and its level
of industrialization, is an important factor.

Russia has to be considered on its own. One should remember that for the Eastern European countries 1989 was a
very positive symbol, the expression of an active struggle to
break free from foreign domination. Russia itself experienced
quite a different process of change. The prime mover, Mr
Gorbachev, had no real idea of the forces he was unleashing.
Gorbachev had a positive vision of the future, an extremely

influential one, as it turned out – to bring the arms race to a halt. By the mid-1980s he had come to see that there was no future for Russia in persisting with the arms competition with the US, or indeed with the Cold War itself. The future, he asserted, would depend upon international cooperation, not a bipolar system. At the time Reagan was taken by surprise. He and many others saw Gorbachev's stance as just another version of Russian hypocrisy, the claim that there should be a 'new world order' simply disguising the fact that Russia was falling far behind the US economically and in terms of weapons development. These factors no doubt did influence Gorbachev's thinking, but it seems clear that he was sincere in the change in orientation he proposed. What he thought it would do, however, was to allow capitalism and Communism to coexist. He didn't foresee that Communism would be overthrown. This is a prime reason why Gorbachev became so unpopular in Russia. He was blamed for most of the problems that arose when the Communist system broke down.

Russia thus didn't experience a 'bourgeois revolution' in the sense in which the Eastern European countries did in 1989. The old party élites in large part simply moved into new economic and political roles. It isn't surprising that the progress of democratization thus far has been relatively limited, while economic development has fallen into the hands of gangster capitalists. Some – like Richard Layard – have written enthusiastically of the economic and political prospects for Russia, even in the short term. I feel much more cautious. The problems Russia faces are daunting. Some seem to think that gangster capitalism will become normalized, much as happened in Chicago after the 1920s. But Chicago was a city in a larger society which already possessed stable political and economic institutions. Gangster capitalism which covers much of the country is something quite different. Much of the capital being accumulated is going into bank accounts elsewhere. The state has fundamental problems in acquiring tax revenue, partly as a result. These have been alleviated to some degree by loans, but the outcome is likely to be an unpayable deficit. Privatization is a much more difficult issue in Russia than in Eastern Europe, because of the sheer scale of some of the enterprises involved and because of the position with the agricultural sector. Agrarian reform is badly needed, but there is no option other than to proceed slowly, partly because of resistance to change and partly because any other path would create millions more unemployed workers.

Russia has vast natural resources, including large stocks of oil and natural gas. It is potentially a wealthy country. But at the moment what I would foresee is the rapid development of certain cities and regions, especially Moscow and its surroundings, with much of the remainder being fairly stagnant. Also, one shouldn't forget the magnitude of the environmental difficulties to be overcome.

Politically there are two problems: whether the state can hold together in the face of further demands for regional autonomy, and how fast and far democratization will go. Each of these questions should be approached in relation to globalization. It isn't just a question of Russia making a successful transition to liberal democracy, but coping with factors affecting even the most mature liberal democratic societies. Like a benign virus, democracy is spreading everywhere, below and above the level of the nation-state. Coping with these pressures in a constructive way isn't going to be easy, to say the least.

Let's now turn to East Asia. Until recently, it seemed as though in Asia what were formally Third World countries were pioneering

*a highly successful form of economic development. Talk of the
'Asian miracle' was everywhere. Many were also speaking of the
coming Pacific Century, including within this vision China as
well as the Asian tiger economies. The crisis in East Asia has
caused them to shift these perspectives. We don't hear quite so
much now about what the Asian miracle has to teach the West.
Where does the 'Asian miracle' stand today?*

I once wrote an article called 'The Perils of Punditry'. It has a
particular poignancy in relation to commentaries on East Asia.
Almost overnight, and with indecent haste, attitudes to the
Asian economies changed. Before 1997, high levels of borrowing, resistance to external investment, and political and
moral authoritarianism were all widely seen as benefits. Now
they are equally widely understood as weaknesses. There is
an element of truth in both perceptions. A set of characteristics which permits rapid development in conditions of linear
modernization can become an obstacle to further development
where reflexive modernization comes into play.

   The tiger economies, of course, differ substantially from one
another, with China being a special case on its own. Events will
no doubt unfold differently in the various countries involved.
Growth rates over the next few years are likely to be lower in all
of them, perhaps even negative in one or two cases. The conditions for successful further development in these countries are
the following: the successful combating of corruption and
clientelism, in the banking sector but also in the large corporations; the extension of democracy, where this means not only
an effective multi-party system but the other forms of democratization we have been discussing; openness to inward investment; and increasing gender equality. The last of these hasn't
often been mentioned in discussions about the future of East
Asia. But I feel it is crucial. There is no way to reflexive mod-

ernization except via greater sexual democracy, with all the problems as well as the opportunities this brings in its wake.

Will the 'Chinese way' continue to generate rapid economic development in that vast country while the Communist Party maintains its tight hold? For what it's worth, I don't think so. Rapid economic development may continue, but democratization will come. From then on in, who knows what will happen? China might revert to a pattern of strong regionalism, combined with high levels of social and regional inequality.

That still leaves two whole areas of the world which we haven't referred to – Latin America and Africa. I don't expect you to be a universal pundit, especially since you've just warned about the dangers of punditry anyway, but could you sketch in a view of where you think overall trends of development in these two continents are leading?

You don't ask easy questions, do you? I'm happy to hazard a few guesses, but I can't claim any special expertise.

One of the most significant changes in Latin America has been precisely increasing democratization – the move away from military dictatorship and other forms of authoritarian rule. Some Latin American countries in the past have oscillated backwards and forwards between military rule, democracy and the reimposition of military government. I think this cycle is now broken. Democratization is a generic process, propelled by wider globalizing forces. Globalization and other related changes have also affected the more established democratic regimes: the long period of 'democratic one-party government' in Mexico, for example, has been brought to an end.

On an economic level, much will depend upon what happens to the three biggest economies, Brazil, Mexico and Argentina. Each is large in world terms: Brazil is number eight as measured in terms of GDP, Mexico sixteen and Argentina eighteen. The economic prospects for Brazil, in spite of relatively low growth rates in recent years, seem good, depending on what happens in the world economy at large. The radical curbing of inflation is a major accomplishment. Brazil has the capacity to become a real economic powerhouse, but the big problem is how to improve the lot of the poor and excluded. Brazil remains a strikingly unequal country as measured against the rest of the top twenty economies. Indeed, one of the most elaborate international comparisons showed inequality in Latin America to be higher than in the US, Europe or Australasia. Dependency theory long having been abandoned, I don't see any obvious solutions on the horizon. The containment of inequality starts from quite a different base from in Europe, and the problems there are difficult enough.

The Mexican crisis had important symbolic value for Latin America. The United States was heavily involved in the bailout mission, but I feel the outcome strengthened the growing independence of Latin America from domination by the North. I see Latin America emerging as more and more of an autonomous area, with an increasingly significant role to play in world affairs. I would like Brazil to become a true world leader alongside the other nations, in the inner circle of the UN. Dependency theory helped isolate Latin America and it is good that the subcontinent is now being drawn more fully into the emerging world society. Political innovations in Chile and elsewhere have set standards for the rest of the world, or at least offered models from which other states and regions can learn.

Over the past twenty years, the time in which the global information economy has become established, sub-Saharan Africa has experienced growth in relative poverty. The facts are well known. I share the view of Manuel Castells, in his *End of Millennium*, that such a deterioration is causally bound up with the very expansion of that global economy. In a more thorough-going way even than was true of the old Soviet bloc, Africa has become excluded from the global information revolution. Castells describes Africa as 'the Fourth World', created by the very breakup of the other three. The impoverishment of Africa is indicated by the fact that whereas it produced over 3 per cent of world exports in 1950, by the early 1990s this had declined to just over 1 per cent. Import ratios also went down. Even including South Africa, African exports have remained largely restricted to primary commodities, especially agricultural products. Overseas borrowing and international aid have become essential components of most of the core African economies. In some countries, for example Mozambique, aid income accounted in 1995 for over 50 per cent of GNP.

The long-term difficulties of Africa are without doubt the fractured legacy of colonialism, with the Cold War serving to worsen the continent's position. The dominance of local state bureaucracies has produced lack of investment, underdeveloped communications and a failure to develop human capital. These factors are self-reinforcing – overseas capital is disinclined to invest in African countries because such investment is quite objectively a very risky affair.

South Africa and Nigeria could in principle unlock the economic prison in which Africa finds itself. Nigeria has some 20 per cent of the total population of Africa south of the Sahara. Yet its prospects at the moment don't look good. State control of the economy, in spite of, or perhaps because of, the oil revenues, has proved a serious barrier to sustained economic development. The Nigerian state is a clear residue of the colonial era and its continuing lack of legitimacy is both cause and effect of the role of the military in government over the past thirty-five years. Nigeria, like many other ex-colonial

State-nation vs. nation-state

states in Africa, is a state-nation. What is needed is not so much the formation of a nation-state as the reform of government within the context of involvement in the world economy.

Some see in South Africa the catalyst which could spark a positive reaction in the rest of the continent and reverse its decline. South Africa is much more highly industrialized than any other sub-Saharan country. In fact, in the early 1990s it accounted for over half the industrial output of the whole of Africa south of the Sahara. Yet it is highly unequal, much more unequal, for instance, even than Brazil. Some studies rate it as having the most unequal income distribution in the world. Income and wealth are overwhelmingly concentrated among the top 10 per cent of the population, nearly all of whom are non-black. In spite of the aspirations of its government, South Africa is more integrated in the external world economy than in Africa as such. It seems unlikely at the moment that South Africa could be the dynamo of an 'African miracle'.

How hopeful are you about the future? Are you in the end an optimist or a pessimist?

The concept of risk, which I've often referred to in this book, to me cuts across optimism and pessimism. Risk is simultaneously the energizing mechanism of our lives and at the heart of the new dilemmas we face. I wouldn't object to Ulrich Beck's characterization of the world in which we live as a 'global risk society'. It is up to us in the next century to strike an effective balance between opportunity and risk.

Centre Left at Centre Stage*

Is there a distinctive position for what Tony Blair has come to call the centre left?

During the run-up to the 1997 election, Martin Jacques and Stuart Hall penned an exasperated article, 'Tony Blair: The Greatest Tory since Margaret Thatcher?' 'With the Tories divided, exhausted and demoralised', they wrote, 'it is still their arguments, their philosophy, their priorities, that are defining the agenda on which New Labour thinks and speaks.' New Labour has shifted so far to the centre that the party represents merely a warmed-over Thatcherism. 'A Blair government', they say, 'promises to be a messy business' – and short-lived, too.

Blair must be as conscious as anyone of the difficulties involved. Many other critics since the election have echoed the criticisms made by Jacques and Hall. The Labour manifesto says, 'We have modernised the Labour Party and we will modernise Britain'. But the first doesn't supply much guidance for the second. It is quite easy to say what 'modernisation' is when

* Originally published in *New Statesman*, May 1997, special edition.

applied to the Labour Party: as applied to an industrial country as a whole, deciding what the word means is much more demanding.

The stakes are high. Twice before in the post-war period the UK has pioneered ideas and policies that have influenced political thought and practice across the world. The first was the creation of the Keynesian welfare state, which Labour did so much to shape. The second was Thatcherism or, more broadly, neo-liberalism. If New Labour has the vision and the courage, it could be the sparking-point for a new political framework of comparable importance and influence to those that went before. For the old 'welfare consensus' is no more, and Blair is right to say there can be no going back to it. Neo-liberalism, however, has not only run out of steam, it was a thoroughly inadequate and self-contradictory political philosophy to begin with – as the Tories found to their cost and Labour will also discover if the party does not advance beyond it.

Has Labour got some way towards establishing a third phase in British politics, or is it simply in the unprincipled muddle that critics such as Jacques and Hall assert?

My response is that the party and the bevy of advisers and intellectuals around it have made a good stab at the task, even if the result so far isn't especially exciting or compelling. The centre-left project as it stands runs as follows. New Labour seeks to think in the long term, as regards labour markets, industry and the fabric of government itself. Investment in human and social capital, in which the state must play a significant part, must complement capital investment of a more orthodox type. Long-termism will be encouraged in corporations via a culture of stakeholding, however that is conceived. Constitutional reform, a desirable feature of modernization in any case, will play its part in developing social capital, because it will increase trust in government. The whole thing will be underpinned morally by an emphasis on the matching of rights with obligations.

There is some force in all of this and it does attempt to create a break with neo-liberalism. Depending on what particular gloss one puts on the project, it implies dragging the UK away from the US model in the direction of something like stakeholder or Rhineland capitalism. I don't want to dispute the importance of investing in human and social capital, and the stakeholding idea is surely of value, albeit a more limited one than its advocates claim. But the party needs to give hard thought to whether its overall perspective is compelling enough to provide a sufficient grasp on the challenges it will confront.

What follows is a few suggestions about how the centre-left project might be fleshed out further. At the risk of sounding didactic, I'll suggest some issues that need to be looked at, but also offer possible answers – mostly these are in the food-for-thought category, for a coherent and persuasive left-of-centre programme is still in the making.

What is the centre left? As I understand it, it is a political standpoint that speaks to the fundamental changes happening in the world, changes that mean the division between left and right no longer has the purchase on reality it once had. New political allegiances and new forms of consensus-building become possible, many of which concern problems that don't have clear-cut left or right solutions. The centre left doesn't preclude radicalism, in fact it seeks to develop the idea of the radical centre. The notion of the radical centre is an oxymoron only if one believes left and right still define all worthwhile ideas and policies in politics. I mean by it that there are political problems which demand radical solutions, but for which wide cross-class support can be mustered.

The centre left continues to draw inspiration from left

values, but accepts that socialism is dead as a theory of economic management and as an interpretation of history. The
main continuing difference between left and right is that those
on the left attach more value to promoting equality and democracy, and believe the state can act to further these.

What are the changes to which the centre left responds?
The dominant influence over our lives is globalization, a phenomenon that as yet is only poorly understood. The word
'globalization' has become so commonplace (although it was
hardly used even ten years ago) that a reaction has set in, with
some arguing that it is more or less a neo-liberal myth. However, we should understand by globalization not just an intensifying of world economic competition, but a shift in the
way we live. We are all learning to adapt to a global cosmopolitan society, with its benefits and changes – a society producing seismic shocks that disrupt familiar institutions, from
marriage and the family through to the nation-state and beyond. Contrary to what many observers say, globalization
makes political decisions more urgent and consequential than
they used to be, not less.

Radical thinking and policy will be necessary to confront
the problems and maximize the opportunities globalization
brings to the fore. The policy issues at the top of Labour's
agenda – including constitutional change, devolution, reform
of the welfare state and the future of the European Union – all
express globalizing influences.

What should the project of modernization be? It is important to recognize that there are now two forms of modernization in play across the world, and in some part they are
in conflict.

What I'll call 'first-phase modernization' refers to modern-
izing processes that take a society, as it were, in a straight line
towards increasing wealth, and where prosperity, security and

2nd phase modernization [handwritten margin note]

improvement in overall quality of life tend to go together. 'Second-phase modernization' – reflexive modernization – happens where these conditions no longer hold, and where modernization means coming to terms with some of its own limits, tensions and difficulties.

Issues raised by second-phase modernization can't be resolved by means of first-phase strategies. Asian economic development thus far, for example, has been linear or first-phase modernization – the more mature Asian economies are hitting serious second-phase problems now. Second-phase modernization does not imply a steady-state or no-growth economy. It is consistent with low-inflation, low-growth targets. It generates increasing prosperity. But it means dealing also with aspects of life either where there is too much rather than too little (e.g. car traffic) or where economic development has proved damaging. It demands an integration with ecological concerns, broadly conceived. The Labour manifesto has a stronger emphasis on environmentalism than previous policy documents, but there is a long way to go. An ecological outlook can help weld together many concerns in a programme of social and economic renewal. Business and ecological groups are increasingly coming to work in tandem, rather than seeing their interests as inevitably opposed; taxation can be moved further in the direction of consumption and away from production; urban and transport policy, seen in an ecological context, connects with a diversity of other policy areas.

New Labour has no overall economic theory. If such a theory can't be Keynesianism and shouldn't be neo-liberalism, what might it be? No one yet has a clear-cut answer, but there is an emerging paradigm that could be of value in shaping the economic orientation of the party. This is the paradigm of what Michael Mandel, a US economist, has called the high-risk economy.

The high-risk economy, which reflects globalized conditions, is one in which, as noted earlier, wealth-creation, security and quality of life become uncoupled. The positive acceptance of uncertainty, and the ability to make successful 'investment' decisions in many areas of life, is increasingly the basis of successful global economic competition. Growth, as Mandel, puts it, is 'fed by forces that intensify uncertainty rather than reduce it'. In the high-risk economy, hunting for the sure thing cannot be an effective strategy in the long run. There is too much available information, entry is easy and competitors abound. Government must help to provide the means of security that people rightly require. We can't and shouldn't try to insulate people against risk. Acceptance of risk is the condition of prosperity (and necessary to confront the ecological and other problems it brings with it). Security needs to be provided instead through insurance. Since the welfare state is in large part a state-run system for managing risks, this consideration is directly relevant to the restructuring of welfare.

The possibilities are many. Take, for example, income averaging. Income averaging means calculating tax liability on average income over three or four years instead of each individual year. It would provide a benefit for those who lost their jobs, or where income dropped markedly (not for those whose incomes rose substantially), without reducing incentives.

How should New Labour approach the problem of unemployment, in some ways the most basic social challenge of the moment? The party's answer couples an active labour-market policy to a traditional goal of full employment. This is also basic in its approach to countering inequality and poverty.

'The best way to tackle poverty', said the manifesto, 'is to help people into jobs – real jobs.' This might seem to be Labour at its strongest, but I would agree with the critics who say that here it is weak. Getting people into jobs doesn't necessarily tackle poverty, as the example of the US shows, and full employment can't mean the same as it did a generation ago. Labour must as a matter of urgency address the debate about the future of work, and should do so in collaboration with the unions. Only a third of the labour force in the UK, excluding those under eighteen and over sixty-five, is working in full-time occupations with stable job security – the basis of old-type 'full employment'. At the same time non-employment (as opposed to unemployment) is achieving a rich diversity of meanings.

This observation is more closely related to problems of inequality than one might imagine. Existing welfare institutions can no longer cope, and in any case need to be reshaped, while further direct income transfers from rich to poor through income tax are not an option. We should look instead for means of redistributing employment, and more generally redistributing work. Government can and should act to do so, on a diversity of fronts. Some of Labour's current policies on reducing long-term unemployment make a contribution to work redistribution, but they are a small bite out of a much larger cherry. The redistribution of work could encompass, among other things: tax incentives for corporations that gear recruitment and job stability to wider social needs; the further expansion of higher education, which, besides its civilizing role, defers entry into or takes people out of the labour market; career-break and career re-entry schemes for a range of age groups; the breakdown of the division between 'men's' and 'women's' jobs; any provisions that encourage men to define themselves more fully in terms of family responsibilities, and that make it easier for women with children to sustain a career.

The party's proposed labour market reforms won't arrest

the drift towards the formation of an underclass. Yet if the 'left' in 'centre left' is to mean anything, this is one point where Labour must make its policies count, and where the party should make a clean break with neo-liberalism. How? There is a lot of thinking to do. There seems good evidence to show that inequality is dysfunctional to economic success in the global market place. On the whole, more unequal societies seem less prosperous (and less healthy) than less unequal societies. Why not build a concerted attack on poverty into a strategy for enhancing overall economic competitiveness? Of course, the fundamental problem to be faced up to is: can anything be done for the have-nots without exerting more control over the prerogatives of the haves?

What moral stance should Labour have?   This still needs some more thinking through. Christianity, strong families and acting tough on crime – the mix has made many Labour supporters uneasy. In fact there is absolutely no need to be a Thatcherite on these issues – a different and more consistent position is possible.

Labour strategists will say talking tough on moral issues has got them where they are. Blair's rise to the top began when he persuaded the public that Labour was no longer soft on crime. Talk of teaching the differences between right and wrong and of strong families is popular. Why drop these things now?

They shouldn't so much be dropped as looked at in a different way, as well as freed from their authoritarian overtones. The Tories try to mix chalk and cheese when simultaneously advocating economic individualism and moral authoritarianism. Blair shouldn't persist with this category mistake. Why speak of modernization in all other contexts save this one? The only feasible project for the centre left is in fact a cosmopolitan one – the recognition that cultural diversity is an inherent part of a globalizing order. There can't be one morality, imposed by any one group; moral issues must be publicly debated and on this basis built in to a sustaining framework of law, including international law. There is no point in advocating a return to traditional moral canons or in proposing a return to the traditional family. It is right to say a new balance between individualism and social obligation must be struck, but moral authoritarianism isn't the way to do it.

Maybe pandering to the prejudices of Little England was necessary to defeat a Conservative Party that had built a populist platform on this basis. A Labour leadership worth its salt must at some point take on these prejudices rather than produce a watered-down form of them. Changes affecting marriage, the family, sexuality and personal life are as profound as those happening in other institutions. They are occurring throughout the industrialized countries and an effective policy platform must be developed to respond positively to them.

Finally, what attitude should Labour take towards the European Union?   I shall offer only a short coda. As a political leader, Blair has a great opportunity to make his mark in Europe – it should be one of his prime concerns over the next few years. The older generation of European leaders is fading and Blair is the most interesting and successful politician of the upcoming generation. To make his presence felt, however, Blair will need to do more than reoccupy the Tory 'empty chair'. The EU should be understood as itself a product of, and a response to, globalization.

From such a perspective, devolution and constitutional reform in the UK, including Scottish home rule and the question of Northern Ireland, can be seen as part of a broader pattern. Globalization pulls upwards and outwards, but simultaneously exerts downward pressure. Local nationalism, and demands for local autonomy more generally, are part and parcel of the processes that create supranational institutions and associations.

'Subsidiarity' in this sense is not primarily a 'policy' of the EU, but a structural condition of its very existence.

Tony Blair now has the chance to lead in Europe in a double sense. He can ensure that being at the heart of Europe means something real and he can lead the way to an influential new programme. The centre left can work towards a political standpoint of some ambition. If this is indeed achieved, history beckons.

The Politics of Risk Society[*]

What do the following have in common: BSE; the troubles at Lloyd's; the Nick Leason affair; global warming; red wine as good for you; declining sperm counts? All reflect a vast swathe of change which we are experiencing in our lives today, bound up with the impact of science and technology on our everyday activities and on the material environment. The modern world, of course, has long been shaped by the influence of science and scientific discovery. As the pace of innovation hots up, however, new technologies penetrate more and more to the core of our lives; and more and more of what we feel and experience comes under the scientific spotlight.

The situation does not lead to increasing certainty about, or security in, the world – in some ways the opposite is true. As Karl Popper above all has shown, science does not produce proof and can never do more than approximate to truth. The founders of modern science believed it would produce knowledge built on firm foundations. Popper supposes, by contrast, that science is built on shifting sands. The first prin-

* Originally published as 'Risk Society: the Context of British Politics' in Jane Franklin, ed., *The Politics of Risk Society* (1997), pp. 23–34.

ciple of scientific advance is that even one's most cherished theories and beliefs are always open to revision. Science is thus an inherently sceptical endeavour, involving a process of the constant revision of claims to knowledge.

The sceptical, mutable nature of science was for a long time insulated from the wider public domain – an insulation which persisted so long as science and technology were relatively restricted in their effects on everyday life. Today, we are all in regular and routine contact with these traits of scientific innovation. The consequences for health of drinking red wine, for example, were once seen by researchers as basically harmful. More recent research indicates that, taken in moderation, the health benefits of red wine outweigh the drawbacks. What will tomorrow's research show? Will it perhaps reveal that red wine is toxic after all?

We don't, and we can't, know – yet all of us, as consumers, have to respond in some way or another to this unstable and complex framework of scientific claims and counterclaims. Living in the UK, should one eat beef? Who can say? The health risk appears to be slight. Yet there is at least the possibility of an outbreak of BSE-related disease five, ten or twenty years from now among the human population.

We don't and can't know – the same applies to a diversity of new risk situations. Take, for instance, declining sperm counts. Some scientific studies make authoritative claims about increasing male infertility, and trace this to the action of environmental toxins. Other scientists, however, dispute the very existence of the phenomenon, let alone the explanations offered to account for it. Global warming is accepted as real by the majority of specialists in the area. Yet there is no shortage of experts who either deny that global warming exists or regard it as produced by long-term climatic fluctuations rather than by the greenhouse effect.

The Lloyd's insurance market seems for the moment to have got over the disastrous financial troubles which have plagued it over the last few years. Such troubles were popularly portrayed as being bound up with class – with the complacent outlook of the 'names' and their brokers. In fact, they had their basic origin in the changing character of risk. Lloyd's was hit by, among other things, findings about the toxic nature of asbestos and by a series of natural disasters – which were possibly not 'natural' at all, but influenced by global climatic change. The number of typhoons, hurricanes and other climatic disturbances happening in the world each year has climbed over the past fifteen years or so. With its massive futures commitments, Lloyd's – in common with other, lesser insurance institutions – could be financially crippled at any time by as yet quite unforeseen negative consequences of new scientific findings or technological changes.

Simon Sebag Montefiore has written an interesting account of the adventures of Nick Leason and Barings Bank. Sebag Montefiore suggests that there are two different ways in which what happened at Barings can be interpreted (much like the events at Lloyd's). On the one hand, there is a class-plus-corruption explanation. According to this view, Barings Bank collapsed because it had a crusty, upper-class management at odds with the demands of a dynamic global economic order.

Sebag Montefiore casts doubt on this explanation. He argues that people working at the outer edges of the financial system, particularly in futures markets – complex markets where deals can be struck over movements in prices which have not yet happened and may never happen – are like astronauts. They have stepped outside the realm of bankers and financial experts – and they have stepped outside without a lifeline. Nick Leason drifted away much too far from any solid ground, but most others are able to keep themselves attached to their space capsule.

Sebag Montefiore has a very arresting phrase to describe this situation. He says Nick Leason and other people like him 'operate at the outer edge of the ordered world, on the barbaric final frontier of modern technology'. In other words, they are involved with systems which even they themselves do not understand, so dramatic is the onrush of change in the new electronic global economy. I think this is right, but the argument can be further generalized. It is not just people like Nick Leason, not just the new financial entrepreneurs, who live at the barbaric outer edge of modern technology. *All* of us now do – and I would take this to be the defining characteristic of what Ulrich Beck calls risk society. A risk society is a society where we increasingly live on a high-technological frontier that no one completely understands and which generates a diversity of possible futures.

The origins of risk society can be traced to two fundamental transformations which are affecting our lives today. Each is connected to the increasing influence of science and technology, although not wholly determined by them. The first transformation can be called the end of nature; and the second the end of tradition.

The end of nature does not mean a world in which the natural environment disappears. It means that there are now few if any aspects of the physical world untouched by human intervention. The end of nature is relatively recent. It has come about over something like the last forty or fifty years, largely as a result of the intensification of technological change noted earlier.

It isn't something, of course, which can be precisely dated, but we can nevertheless roughly plot when the end of nature happened. It happened when a transition came about from the sorts of anxiety people used to have about nature to a new set of worries. For hundreds of years, people worried about what nature could do to us – earthquakes, floods, plagues, bad harvests and so on. At a certain point, somewhere over the past fifty years or so, we stopped worrying so much about what nature could do to us, and we started worrying much more about what we have done to nature. That transition makes one major point of entry into risk society. It is a society which lives after nature.

However, it is also a society which lives after tradition. To live after the end of tradition is essentially to be in a world where life is no longer lived as fate. For many people – and this is still a source of class division in modern societies – diverse aspects of life were established by tradition as fate. It was the fate of a woman to be involved in a domestic milieu for much of her life, to have children and look after the house. It was the fate of men to go out to work, to work until they retired and then – quite often soon after retirement – essentially to fade away. We no longer live our lives in this way, a transition which Ulrich Beck calls individualization. A society which lives after nature and after tradition is really very different from the earlier form of industrial society – the basis for the development of the core intellectual traditions of Western culture.

To analyse what risk society is, one must make a series of distinctions. First of all, we must separate risk from hazard or danger. Risk is not, as such, the same as hazard or danger. A risk society is not intrinsically more dangerous or hazardous than pre-existing forms of social order. It is instructive in this context to trace out the origins of the term 'risk'. Life in the Middle Ages was hazardous; but there was no notion of risk and there doesn't seem in fact to be a notion of risk in any traditional culture. The reason for this is that dangers are experienced as given. Either they come from God, or they come simply from a world which one takes for granted. The idea of risk is bound up with the aspiration to control and particularly with the idea of controlling the future.

This observation is important. The idea of 'risk society' might suggest a world which has become more hazardous, but this is not necessarily so. Rather, it is a society increasingly preoccupied with the future (and also with safety), which generates the notion of risk. The idea of risk, interestingly, was first used by Western explorers when they ventured into new waters in their travels across the world. From exploring geographical space, it came to be transferred to the exploration of time. The word refers to a world which we are both exploring, and seeking to normalize and control. Essentially, 'risk' always has a negative connotation, since it refers to the chance of avoiding an unwanted outcome. But it can quite often be seen in a positive light, in terms of the taking of bold initiatives in the face of a problematic future. Successful risk-takers, whether in exploration, in business or in mountaineering, are widely admired.

We should distinguish risk from hazard, but we must also make a distinction between two kinds of risk. The first two hundred years of the existence of industrial society were dominated by what one might call *external risk*. External risk, expressed in down-to-earth terms, is risk of events that may strike individuals unexpectedly (from the outside, as it were), but that happen regularly enough and often enough in a whole population of people to be broadly predictable, and so insurable. There are two kinds of insurance associated with the rise of industrial society: the private insurance company and public insurance, which is the predominant concern of the welfare state.

The welfare state became the left's project in the post-1945 period – it became seen above all as a means of achieving social justice and income redistribution. By and large, however, it did not originate as such. It developed as a security state, a way of protecting against risk, where collective rather than private insurance was necessary. Like early forms of private insurance, it was built on the presumption of external risk. External risk can be fairly well calculated – one can draw up actuarial tables and decide on that basis how to insure people. Sickness, disablement, unemployment were treated by the welfare state as 'accidents of fate', against which insurance should be collectively provided.

A world which lives after nature and after the end of tradition is one marked by a transition from external to what I call *manufactured risk*. Manufactured risk is risk created by the very progression of human development, especially by the progression of science and technology. Manufactured risk refers to new risk environments for which history provides us with very little previous experience. We often don't really know what the risks are, let alone how to calculate them accurately in terms of probability tables.

Manufactured risk is expanding in most dimensions of human life. It is associated with a side of science and technology which the early theorists of industrial society by and large did not foresee. Science and technology create as many uncertainties as they dispel – and these uncertainties cannot be 'solved' in any simple way by yet further scientific advance. Manufactured uncertainty intrudes directly into personal and social life – it isn't confined to more collective settings of risk. In a world where one can no longer simply rely on tradition to establish what to do in a given range of contexts, people have to take a more active and risk-infused orientation to their relationships and involvements.

The rise of risk society has several interesting consequences – which should concern anyone who has taken an interest in the BSE debate in Britain and Continental Europe, or in fact in any of the episodes I mentioned at the beginning of this discussion.

As manufactured risk expands – or, if you like, as we live more and more in a risk society, in Ulrich Beck's terms – there is a new riskiness to risk. In a social order in which new technologies are chronically affecting our lives, and an almost endless revision of taken-for-granted ways of doing things ensues, the future becomes ever more absorbing, but at the same time opaque. There are few direct lines to it, only a plurality of 'future scenarios'.

We recently saw the tenth anniversary of the nuclear disaster at the Chernobyl plant. No one knows whether hundreds or very many more people have been affected by the Chernobyl fall-out. The long-term effects will in any case be difficult to chart, because if they exist they are likely to be diffuse. We are altering the environment, and the patterns of life we follow, almost constantly. Even many apparently benign habits or innovations could turn sour – just as, conversely, risks can often be overestimated. Take the example of smoking. Smoking was encouraged by doctors up to some thirty or so years ago as a means of relaxation. No one knew the time bomb which the practice of smoking was stirring up. The BSE episode might have an opposite outcome. Perhaps it will turn out that humans are not affected. It is characteristic of the new types of risk that it is even disputed whether they exist at all.

In risk society there is a new moral climate of politics, one marked by a push-and-pull between accusations of scaremongering on the one hand and of cover-ups on the other. A good deal of political decision-making is now about managing risks – risks which do not originate in the political sphere, yet have to be politically managed. If anyone – government official, scientific expert or lay person – takes any given risk seriously, he or she must announce it. It must be widely publicized, because people must be persuaded that the risk is real – a fuss must be made about it. However, if a fuss is indeed created and the risk turns out to be minimal, those involved will be accused of scaremongering.

Suppose on the other hand that the authorities decide that the risk is not very great, as the British government initially did with BSE. In this case, the government says: we've got the backing of scientists here; there isn't much risk, we can go on as we did before. Yet if things turn out otherwise, then of course they will be accused of a cover-up.

Paradoxically, scaremongering may be necessary to reduce risks we face – yet if it is 'successful' in this sense, it appears as just that, scaremongering. The case of AIDS is an example. Suppose governments and experts make great public play with the risks associated with unsafe sex, to get people to change their sexual behaviour. Suppose then that many people do change their sexual behaviour and AIDS does not spread nearly as much as originally predicted. The response is likely to be: why were you scaring everyone like that? This sort of political dilemma becomes routine in risk society, but there is no easily available way of confronting it. For as I mentioned earlier, even whether there are any risks at all is likely to be controversial. We just cannot know beforehand when we are actually 'scaremongering' and when we are not.

Third, the emergence of risk society is not wholly about the avoidance of hazards, for reasons also given previously. Risk has positive aspects to it. Risk society, looked at positively, is one in which there is an expansion of choice. Now obviously choice is differentially distributed according to class and income. As nature and tradition release their hold, for instance, some otherwise infertile women can pay to have children through the use of new reproductive technologies, whereas others cannot. We know that in detraditionalized social settings some women live in poverty after divorce, whereas others achieve a more rewarding life than they could have done before. Technological innovation usually expands the domain of choice; as does the disappearance of tradition. As customary ways of doing things become problematic, people must choose in many areas which used to be governed by taken-for-granted norms. Eating is an example: there are no traditional diets any more.

The advent of risk society has strong implications for rethinking the political agenda in this country and elsewhere. The emergence of manufactured risk presumes a new politics because it presumes a reorientation of values and the strategies relevant to pursuing them. There is no risk which can even be described without reference to a value. That value may be simply the preservation of human life, although it is usually more complex. When there is a clash of the different types of risk, there is a clash of values and a directly political set of questions.

All of these issues are highly relevant to Tony Blair's project for New Labour. Blair is often spoken of as a conservative, who is destroying the values and perspectives of the left. I think it could be said, on the contrary, that he is one of the few leading politicians actively trying to come to terms with the profound changes affecting local life and the global order. In that sense, his orientation could fairly be described as a radical one. However, the idea of modernization, which Blair treats as central, needs to be rethought.

Modernization, as Blair uses the term, means bringing Britain up to date. Tony Blair has been the archetypical modernizer within the Labour Party; but more fundamentally, he wants to modernize British institutions – modernization carrying the connotation in this country that Britain lags behind other industrial societies in various key respects. Now this is a bit like the first explanation that Sebag Montefiore mentions for the collapse of Barings Bank – crusty old institutions which have lost their relevance to the modern world.

That there is something in the project of modernization, thus understood, can be seen by anyone who sets foot in the House of Lords. In risk society, however, modernization means something different. Risk society is industrial society which has come up against its own limitations, where those limitations take the form of manufactured risk. Modernization in this sense cannot simply be 'more of the same'.

We should distinguish here between simple and reflexive modernization. Simple modernization is old-type, unilinear modernization; reflexive modernization, by contrast, implies coming to terms with the limits and contradictions of the modern order. These are obvious in new domains of politics associated with various sorts of social movement. They are obvious in motorway protests, in animal rights demonstrations and in many of the food scares. Second-phase modernization – modernization as reflexive modernization – will not look like first-phase modernization. There is an opportunity, I think, for political debate in the UK to leap ahead of that in many other European countries in this respect, and I would like to see this happen. Reflexive modernization, like risk more generally, is by no means wholly a negative prospect and offers many possibilities for positive political engagement.

Our relationship to science and technology today is different from that characteristic of early industrial society. In Western society, for some two centuries, science functioned as a sort of tradition. Scientific knowledge was supposed to overcome tradition but actually became a taken-for-granted authority in its own right. It was something which most people respected, but was external to their lives. Lay people 'took' opinions from the experts.

The more science and technology intrude into our lives, the less this external perspective holds. Most of us – including government authorities and politicians – have, and have to have, a much more dialogic or engaged relationship with science and technology than used to be the case. We cannot simply 'accept' the findings which scientists produce, if only because scientists so frequently disagree with one another, particularly in situations of manufactured risk. And everyone now recognizes the essentially sceptical character of science described earlier. Whenever someone decides what to eat, what to have for breakfast, whether to drink decaffeinated or ordinary coffee, that person takes a decision in the context of conflicting, changeable scientific and technological information.

There is no way out of this situation – we are all caught up in it, even if we choose to proceed 'as if in ignorance'. Politics must give some institutional form to this dialogical engagement because at the moment it concerns only special-interest groups, who mostly struggle outside the main political domain. We do not currently possess institutions which allow us to monitor technological change. We might have prevented the BSE debacle if a public dialogue had already been established about technological change and its problematic consequences. Enoch Powell apparently remarked that nothing affects our lives as much as technological change, and he was right – yet such change is completely outside the democratic system. More public means of engaging with science and technology wouldn't do away with the quandary of scaremongering versus cover-ups, but it might allow us to mute some of its more damaging consequences.

These considerations are relevant to rethinking the welfare state. The welfare state was founded against the backdrop of a society where nature was still nature and tradition was still tradition. This is obvious, for example, in the gender provisions in the post-1945 welfare state, which simply presumed the continuity of the 'traditional family'. It is obvious in terms of the growth of the National Health Service, which was set up as a response mechanism to illness understood as external risk.

In a world of more active engagement with health, with the body, with marriage, with gender, with work – in an era of manufactured risk – the welfare state cannot continue in the form in which it developed in the post-1945 settlement. The crisis of the welfare state is not purely fiscal, it is a crisis of risk management in a society dominated by a new type of risk.

These observations are relevant to class division. J.K. Galbraith's so-called 'culture of contentment' was a bit of a shooting star – there is no culture of contentment. One reason why many middle-class and professional groups have opted out of public welfare schemes is bound up with a certain attitude towards risk management. The middle classes detach themselves from public provision and in a certain sense they are right to do so, because that provision was geared to a different interpretation and situation of risk. When people have a more active orientation to their lives, they also have to have more active attitudes to risk management, so it is not surprising that those who can afford it tend to opt out of existing welfare systems.

Political debate needs to take much greater account of the significance of ecological debates, themselves deeply bound up with the advance of manufactured risk. Ecological questions precisely reflect a world living after nature and after tradition. Many forms of lifestyle politics develop which have no precedent in the earlier type of industrial society. Protesters some while ago made a great deal of fuss about veal calves being transported to the Continent in constrained and artificial conditions. Their critics called them sentimental. Yet in the light of the experience of BSE, everyone can see that this wasn't just sentiment. The protests reflected a latent sense of what can happen when the industrial production of food becomes distanced from nature – or what used to be nature. A moral commitment to animal rights is, in a certain sense, a hard-edged politics. After all, even measured in narrow economic terms, the BSE crisis has been a disaster. Calculations put the cost to the British economy at £6 billion or perhaps even more.

Risk society is not the same as postmodernism. Postmodern interpretations see politics as at an end – political power simply loses its significance with the passing of modernity. Yet modernity does not disappear with the arrival of manufactured risk; rather modernization, which continues, takes on new meanings and subtleties. Reflexive modernization presumes and generates a politics. That politics cannot unfold completely outside the parliamentary domain. Social movements and special-interest groups cannot supply what parliamentary politics offers – the means of reconciling different interests with one another, and also of balancing different risks in relation to one another. The issues I have discussed demand to be brought more directly into the political arena. A party able to address them cogently would be in a prime position in the political encounters that will unfold over the coming few years.

Beyond Chaos and Dogma . . . *

George Soros, the man who broke the Bank of England, talks with Anthony Giddens about the need for a global polity to regulate the world economy

ANTHONY GIDDENS   *I thought we'd begin by discussing the sources of the idea of 'reflexivity' and whether we mean the same thing by it. I mean by it that ideas people have about the social world, about themselves, their future and the conditions of their lives, are not just ideas about an independently 'given' world – they constantly enter the world which they describe. As they do so they change that world – sometimes quite dramatically.*

GEORGE SOROS   I agree with this view. I see reflexivity as a two-way connection between what we think and what happens in the world. And of course there isn't such a two-way connection in nature. It only happens in society, where we act on the basis of our view of the world and our actions determine the outcome, and so shape what that world actually is.

All human life is reflexive in this sense. But to me reflexivity also has a historical element: modern society is distinguished by increasing reflexivity. The main reason is that our lives are deter-

* Originally published in *New Statesman*, 31.10.97.

mined less and less by the fixities of tradition and nature. In many areas of social life decisions must be taken about events which were previously just 'given' – and we take decisions recognizing that these will shape the decisions of others. That's what futures markets are really: they're a kind of continual reflection of risk, folded upon risk, folded upon risk.

This also applies to values. It wouldn't be true to say we have values that are separate from the increasingly reflexive nature of the world – values are directly involved in it, because we live in a world where we have to decide what values to hold, as individuals, and in a democracy, collectively – essentially through reflexive discourse. In more traditional cultures those values are more given.

But can you live with such reflexivity? I am all in favour of pursuing knowledge, or not even knowledge, but understanding, but I worry whether we can live with this knowledge, whether society can survive, without a sense of right and wrong which is common, so that people agree on it. Maybe we should go just one step back from reflexivity, because in my mind, reflexivity is intimately connected with fallibility. That is to say, our view of the world is inherently inadequate, it doesn't correspond to the world, because we are part of the world in which we live, and being part of it we cannot possibly understand it the way it really is. So there is a reality, but it's impossible for us to know it in its entirety. There are elements of it we can know, but we can't know it all, because some of it is contingent on what we think. Fallibility and reflexivity are sister concepts, because if you could base your decisions on knowledge, reflexivity wouldn't exist.

I use two concepts of fallibility. The broad concept is that there is a divergence between our views of social and human phenomena and the phenomena as they occur. The sharper notion is that all our concepts – both our ideas about the world and our institutions – are flawed. They are distorted, misconceived, or inadequate in not covering all aspects of the situations; or at least they may be appropriate at one moment of time, but will not continue to be so because of the reflexive connection – reflexivity will make them inadequate with the passage of time. They are time-bound.

This leads to a critical mode of thinking: if you recognize fallibility you have to be critical about all statements, you have to question if they are true or false, if they are applicable, in what conditions they are applicable; you have to look for the flaw. And that works well in the financial markets, because it leads you to look for the flaw and it allows you to adjust your position in the markets.

When people have lots of information, they get used to assessing that information and looking at it fairly critically, because there's no other way to live. The question is, how deeply can that attitude go? Because if you take medical information – whether we should eat butter or margarine, whether we should take this pill or that pill, whether we should drink red wine, two glasses a day, or whether we shouldn't touch alcohol – you can't maintain a continual critical involvement with all of that. You must have some sort of life patterns or habits. What most people do is sustain a generalized attitude of critical engagement but also put it to one side and get on with their lives. And in a way, that's what we have to do in the society at large.

We can't really live in a totally open way, and you can see . . .

. . . that would be chaos, wouldn't it, really?

Yes, that's the extreme. So you need to bound it, to have some discipline, some values, to guide you in this potentially chaotic world. The range of possibilities is much greater if reality is not given but is part of one's own creation. And many people in this tremendously open world close themselves down in a space of their own and get quite far removed from it. So where this leads me to is that this open society is a precarious state of affairs, which is threatened from both sides. It's threatened by the imposition of dogma, fundamentalism . . .

. . . And chaos on the other side.

Chaos vs Dogma

And chaos on the other side.

It seems to me all of our lives are like that now, sandwiched in this dilemma.

Yes, as I said, there is a question whether we can live with this knowledge of reflexivity, because when you have that knowledge, and everybody else in the market has that knowledge, markets become inherently unstable, there is nothing to hold them. They can move in unexpected ways and become chaotic. I'm afraid that the prevailing view, which is one of extending the market mechanism to all domains, has the potential of destroying society. Unless we review our concept of markets, our understanding of markets, they will collapse, because we are creating global markets, global financial markets, without understanding their true nature. We have this false theory that markets, left to their own devices, tend towards equilibrium. It's not, fortunately, believed in practice – I mean, there are financial authorities who know that markets are not stable, and they try to maintain stability by exercising controls. For example, there is a certain degree of cooperation between the central banks. But I would say

the three major central banks operate with somewhat different ideologies. The Americans have a pretty good understanding of reflexivity, instability – [Alan] Greenspan, [Lawrence]
Summers and [Robert] Rubin – these are people in whom I
have confidence, they understand markets about as well as
one can. In Japan, on the other hand, you've got a set of
people who think they can manipulate the markets to achieve
social and economic goals. They are coming a cropper. They
are in a crisis. They know manipulation got them into a crisis, but they want to manipulate their way out of it. They are
too hands-on and believe too much in their power to control
the market.

The Germans, by contrast, err on the side of non-interven-
tion: they have an absolute value, namely the stability of the
currency. So you have an unstable system, with three major
currencies fluctuating against each other, and not finding any
equilibrium. The yen, for example, at one point went from 72
to the dollar to 127 to the dollar, more than a 50 per cent
move. That's a tremendous dislocation. At the same time Japan's financial structure came close to a meltdown. So markets get quite far from equilibrium. Now, they do it without
necessarily causing a collapse, the breakdown of the system;
these fluctuations occur within the system. There is no tendency towards equilibrium within the system, but the system
still survives.

Well, has survived so far.

It has survived only with intervention: the authorities have
come to the rescue. The instability causes winners and losers;
people who benefit from it and people who lose by it. If the
fluctuation becomes too big people may opt out of the system, or be unable to meet their obligations. Then you can
have a breakdown. It will come through political and eventu-

ally military events, rather than events merely in the financial markets . . .

Can we talk a little more about the political and economic limits of a market economy? There have been two main phases in the evolution of post-war political and economic systems. First there was the welfare state consensus lasting up to the late 1970s, based essentially on fairly co-ordinated national economies – and, I think, on fairly stable lifestyle habits. Keynesianism was the prime economic theory of the expanding welfare state. That was succeeded by a phase of intensifying globalization, accompanied by the rise of Thatcherism or neo-liberalism. Because of the extreme emphasis it puts on markets, it is subject to all the problems just mentioned. The question is, what lies beyond it? We're looking for a theory of a society which is a globalizing society, where market forces are very important, but can be reconciled with social cohesion and a measure of social justice as well as with an open, cosmopolitan community.

So far neo-liberal theory remains dominant. Hopefully the flaws in it will be recognized before it actually produces some sort of collapse.

What might we put in its place?

I am thinking about it. What global competition has done has been to benefit capital at the expense of labour, and to benefit financial capital to the detriment of fixed investments. Because capital is more mobile than labour, and financial capital is most mobile of all, more mobile than direct investment.

That's what's destroyed the old welfare state consensus, because that was based on a balance of capital and labour.

That's right. This destroyed the basis of the welfare state, because you can't tax capital easily, and the more you impose taxes, capital will go somewhere else. And so high-tax countries suffer, because capital flees. This is the crisis facing Continental Europe and the crisis from which Britain has been saved by Margaret Thatcher. I hate to say this because I'm not a fan of hers, but she believed in the markets and demolished a lot of the protectionism, the social protections that existed, which resulted in attracting capital to Britain. The British economy has revived because of the inflow of Japanese and other foreign capital which used Britain as the gateway to Europe.

Wouldn't you say it's revived at considerable social cost?

Oh yes. With the accumulation of wealth there comes increasing social division, and the majority of people don't benefit from the global economy, even though we are all getting richer as countries, as a globe – there are also tremendous benefits from technological advance and so on. So there are a lot of good things going on, but also a lot of bad things. We have to deal with the bad things, otherwise there will be an opting out. Right now we are not anywhere near a revolution, except perhaps in France.

I don't think so – for a revolution, you've got to have an alternative.

Yes, and you don't have socialism, socialism is dead. So the alternative is going to be nationalism. You can see it clearly. The economy, this machine, is a global machine. Capital can move from country to country. If you impose certain levels of social security, you price yourself out of global markets and capital doesn't come. The Le Pens of this world are offering an alternative, one version of fundamentalism. Most people recognize it's not a viable alternative, that by opting out you will hurt yourself much more. And protectionism purely on a French national basis is impossible, because France as a national economy is no longer viable. You could have, conceivably, European protectionism, a fortress Europe. But I don't think that's practical.

I don't think it's even possible.

I don't think so either, because Britain and other like-minded countries would never be part of that. Any attempt to opt out of the global system is liable to release destructive forces that can't be contained. So there's no constructive escape. The only way is to try to correct the inequalities by means of international cooperation. For instance, harmonization of taxes: in Germany, people don't feel obliged to keep their savings in the country so they send them to Luxembourg, where the withholding tax is not in effect. Eventually there will have to be tax harmonization within Europe that would impose tax in Luxembourg. But this is still utopian, because you can't even harmonize within Europe, so how could we harmonize on a world-wide basis? Yet when absolutely necessary it can be done.

We will eventually have to have international regulation of markets. We might benefit from eliminating certain kinds of option from derivatives, because they are destabilizing. So if we are looking for the next positive approach, it has to be a conceptual change, accepting reflexivity and recognizing the need to keep markets stable, to impose some degree of regulation and supervision, and to find a political extension to match the extension of the markets – some international political cooperation to match the globalization of markets. Because what is lacking is the ability of society to impose constraints on the market. The problem is that the inequality can only be corrected on a national basis, and the economy has a global form. It's not trade that makes it global, it is the movement of capital. So somewhere the accumulation of capital has to be tapped, to provide the basis for social insurance. And that's a tough sell.

Risks, Scares, Nightmares*

Consider the following list of precautions. Continually monitor the content of any water you drink: water from any source can be contaminated; do not assume bottled water is safe, especially if bottled in plastic; distil your water at home, since most public water supplies are contaminated. Take care over what you eat. Avoid fish, which is a prime source of contamination, as well as animal fats, whether in cheese, butter or meat; buy organically grown fruits and vegetables or raise your own; minimize contact between plastic and food. Mothers should consider avoiding breast-feeding, because this exposes babies to a high level of contaminants. Wash your hands frequently during the course of each day: contaminants vaporize and settle on any indoor surface, where they are picked up by those who touch them. Do not use any insecticides around the house or in the garden – avoid the homes of those who do. Don't buy produce from a shop or supermarket without checking whether they fog their goods with pesticides, as is common practice. Stay away from golf courses, which have become heavily contaminated, more so even than farmland.

* Originally published in *London Review of Books*, 5.9.96.

Advice about how to survive in the aftermath of a nuclear war? One might be forgiven for thinking so. But this intimidating list of dos and don'ts comes from the new book by Theo Colborn and colleagues, which investigates the damage done to the body by toxic chemicals. If she is right, something of a global holocaust may await us. Not only have entire animal populations been wiped out by becoming unable to reproduce: a whole series of disturbing biological defects is already observable among humans, and these are likely to become more and more damaging in the near future.

Theo Colborn is a wildlife biologist who has brought together diverse pieces of research reporting endocrine disruption in different species of animals. One of her fellow authors is a zoologist; the other is a journalist, for this is a book designed to alert a popular audience to a new range of risks. It carries a foreword by Al Gore, in which he compares the work to that classic of the environmentalist movement, Rachel Carson's *The Silent Spring*, published some thirty years ago. Carson analysed the toxic effects of the spreading use of industrial chemicals, showing how these were accumulating in the soil, as well as in animal and human bodies. *Our Stolen Future* takes up where Carson left off, drawing on large amounts of scientific evidence which have since been gathered.

As her subtitle (*A Scientific Detective Story*) makes clear, Colborn sees her work as tracking down the clues to a puzzling and elusive menace. Her trail starts with birds, otters and fish. Field specialists have been coming up with some bizarre findings in recent years. Florida eagles have become largely sterile; otters have disappeared in some areas of Britain where they were once plentiful; herring gulls living around Lake Ontario have been hatching chicks with grotesque deformities. From around the world other wildlife reports, covering many species, disclose the sudden disappearance of animal populations, impaired fertility, damaged sexual organs and other unexplained physical abnormalities.

And what of ourselves? Colborn picks up here on the celebrated research of Niels Skakkebaek in Denmark. Skakkebaek was one of the first to investigate possible connections between the rate of testicular cancer and a drop in sperm counts. He and his co-workers collected material from over sixty studies carried out around the world. They found that average sperm counts had fallen by almost a half between 1938 and 1990, while the level of testicular cancer had risen sharply. The research survey also suggested that other genital abnormalities were increasing substantially among boys and male teenagers.

The common denominator, Colborn argues, is the ubiquitous influence of hormone-disrupting chemicals in the environment. Most attention thus far has focused on the toxic effects of DDT, the PCBs (polychlorinated biphenyls) and dioxin. According to Colborn, however, over fifty synthetic chemicals, produced commercially, are known to disrupt the endocrine system in one way or another. These differ from naturally occurring oestrogens because they accumulate in the body and are transmitted from parents to their young. They are common in plastics, detergents, sprays and cleaning agents.

Pervasive though they are, synthetic chemicals are for the most part relatively recent. New techniques developed during World War II led to an explosion in their production and use. There are more than a hundred thousand synthetic chemicals on the market and a thousand new ones are introduced every year. Very little is known about their possible effects, even in the laboratories where they undergo tests before being made commercially available. Pesticides are a particularly important category, since they are deliberately dispersed into the environment and are designed to be biologically active. Many include compounds that have been shown to be endocrine disrupters. Five billion pounds of pesticides are spread in the US alone each year – not only in the countryside but in schools, business premises and homes.

While their implications are apocalyptic, the conclusions drawn by Colborn are inevitably tentative. We don't know for certain how serious the contaminant effects are and there are no control groups to turn to, precisely because synthetic chemicals are so widespread. Researchers have looked for control groups among people in remote Inuit villages beyond the Arctic Circle: they found high levels of contamination even there.

Those concerned to safeguard animal and human health, Colborn says, will have to act on information that is less than perfect, for it is possible that the synthetic chemicals are threatening the survival of humanity by destroying the reproductive capacity of the species. That outcome may be very unlikely but we should recognize, Colborn points out, that we are 'flying blind'. In the course of this century, science and technology have penetrated our lives, the animal world and the physical environment to an unprecedented degree. 'These alterations amount to a great global experiment – with humanity and all life on earth as the unwitting subjects . . . We design new technologies at a dizzying pace and deploy them on an unprecedented scale around the world long before we can begin to fathom their possible impact on the global system or ourselves.'

According to Colborn, the first step of any response must be to phase out hormone-displacing chemicals. The use of pesticides must be radically curtailed. We must also move to restrict the continual introduction of new synthetic compounds: indeed we should consider banning the manufacture and release of synthetic chemicals altogether. The National Academy of Sciences in the US has set up an expert panel to assess the threats. Colborn and a group of other interested scientists have produced a 'consensus statement', detailing policies which might improve risk-assessment and begin to curb the 'chemical assault' on the environment.

What are we to make of all this? Colborn's work epitomizes some key dilemmas which all of us face in a world where low-probability, high-consequence risks abound. The most disturbing threats we confront are instances of 'manufactured risk' – they derive from the uncontained advance of science and technology. Science is supposed to make the world more predictable. Often it does. At the same time, it creates new uncertainties – many of them global in character – which by and large we cannot use past experience to resolve.

Manufactured risk is generated by the onrush of science and technology, but both are also necessary to any attempt we make to analyse and cope with it. We can't simply 'turn against science', as some New Age prophets are prone to do – many of the new risks we face are invisible without the diagnostic tools of science. Yet risk assessment can't simply be placed in the hands of scientific experts. All forms of risk calculation and coping strategy imply a consideration of values and desired ways of life. They also have a critical bearing on systems of power and vested interests. Very large economic interests are bound up with the production and marketing of synthetic chemicals. The chemical industry is apparently setting aside millions of pounds to counter the findings of *Our Stolen Future* – the finding that sperm counts are on the decline has already been called into question by research the industry has funded.

A characteristic of the new situations of risk is that the facts of the matter are normally in question and the experts disagree. This is no doubt partly because of the resistance of vested interests, but it is also a result of the novel character of manu-

factured risk. Bruce Ames, a professor of biochemistry at
Berkeley, is one of those who pooh-pooh Colborn's worries:
the effects of synthetic oestrogens, he states in a manner that
doesn't recognize doubt, are minuscule compared to those that
occur naturally, even if the traces of synthetic compounds last
longer in the body. Both Colborn and Ames are respected
scientists.

The generalizing of manufactured risk produces a new moral
climate in which decision-making is dogged by accusations
of scaremongering, on the one hand, and cover-ups, on the
other. *Our Stolen Future* is a perfect case. The scientific evidence which Colborn has gathered is partial and inconclu-
sive, as she herself stresses. Critics will say, and have already
said: don't scare the public when your findings are so incom-
plete. She answers: we have to scare people, because otherwise nothing will get done, and because we have to be safe
rather than sorry.

So far as I can see, there is no easily available exit from this
conundrum. Environmentalists might point to the 'precautionary principle' as a basis for strategy. This means err-
ing on the side of caution when considering technical innovations, and placing the burden of proof on the producer
rather than the victim. With most cases of manufactured risk,
however, the precautionary principle, doesn't help very much.
For, as in the case of hormone-disrupting chemicals, the damage – if indeed it exists – has already been done. Moreover,
testing for long-term effects is impossible and items tested
in isolation may have toxic effects in combination with other
substances.

Governments, regulatory agencies and citizens' groups have
to walk a tightrope when they react to risk. Scaremongering
may often be necessary, but it also tends to undercut itself.
Reluctance to create scares, on the other hand, or bowing to

the influence of vested interests, will inevitably produce an-
gry talk of cover-ups.

In many instances lay individuals can't, or won't, wait for
regulatory bodies to make up their minds about levels and
types of risk. We must all make our own assessments, on the
level of everyday life. In so doing, we must cope with the shifting and contested character of scientific knowledge and with
the media hype which accompanies the diagnosis of new risks
– a tall order. Would anyone actually adopt the whole raft of
precautions I noted earlier? Few surely would or could. Moreover, risks coming from hormone-disrupting chemicals are only
one type among a plurality of risks to be considered and
weighed. Eating a good deal of fish is said by nutritionists to
reduce the risk of heart problems, yet Colborn advises against
fish because of widespread contamination. That said, doing
nothing – just letting things slide – is not possible. In a society which, for better or worse, has radically transformed the
natural environment, we can no longer 'let nature decide'.